Write like Issa:
A Haiku How-To

David G. Lanoue

Copyright © 2017 by David G. Lanoue

HaikuGuy.com

New Orleans, Louisiana, USA

All rights reserved.

ISBN-10: 0-9912840-7-0
ISBN-13: 978-0-9912840-7-8

The cover art shows a page of Issa's calligraphy
from *Waga haru shu* (1811).

Write like Issa:
A Haiku How-To

FOR THE SAKE OF HAIKU

TABLE OF CONTENTS

Foreword: This Book, How It Came About,
    and How to Use It 6

Introduction: Why Issa?. 8

Lesson 1. Compassion as a Way of
    Perception, Consciousness, and Art 10

Lesson 2. Childlike Vision: The Joy and
    Necessity of Unlearning 31

Lesson 3. Comic Vision, Cosmic Jokes 45

Lesson 4. Bold Subjectivity: The "I" Has It . . . 63

Lesson 5. Imagine Going Deeper 77

Lesson 6. Answer Issa in Kind 89

Conclusion: For the Sake of Haiku 102

Notes 104

Publication Credits 116

About the Author 121

Foreword: THIS BOOK, HOW IT CAME ABOUT, AND HOW TO USE IT

I'VE HAD THE PLEASURE of leading "Write like Issa" workshops ten times so far, at . . .

- Haiku Society of America (HSA) conference, Seattle, Washington, June 22, 2013;
- Haiku Holiday retreat, Chapel Hill, North Carolina, April 26, 2014;
- HSA conference, New York City, September 27, 2014;
- Arkansas Haiku Society meeting, Hot Springs, Arkansas, November 1, 2014;
- Reno Buddhist Church, Reno, Nevada, November 15, 2014;
- HSA conference, Washington D.C., December 6, 2014;
- HSA and the Haiku Poets of Northern California joint meeting, Santa Rosa, California, July 19, 2015;
- Yukei Tekei Association conference, Asilomar, California, November 13, 2015;
- Southern California Haiku Study Group, Pasadena, August 20, 2016;
- HSA conference, St. Simons Island, Georgia, April 22, 2017.

Each iteration of the workshop, snowflake-like, was unique—partly because different participants brought different life experiences and insights to the table, and partly because in each workshop I relied on different, randomly chosen examples from Issa to spark discussion and exploration.

The poets who attended and contributed to the ten workshops were instrumental to their success. Therefore, when I came up with the idea of sharing what they and I learned in book form, I decided that for such a book to be as useful as the workshops were, it would need to include voices other than my own and Issa's. I put out a call for submissions by workshop participants and by other poets around the world who are, at least in part, modeling what they do in their art of haiku on the example of the unique poet of early modern Japan who went by the penname Issa: "Cup-of-Tea." By including their haiku alongside those of Cup-of-Tea's, I hope that the present book will be as lively and as creatively stimulating as the workshops were and (if I have the privilege of giving more of them) will be.

As you prepare to move through these lessons, I invite and encourage you to do so actively—as if you were physically present at a workshop. Keep your favorite writing technology nearby, whether pen or keyboard, and be ready to scribble or type your ideas, your discoveries, and—with a bit of luck—your Issa-inspired haiku.

Happy writing!

Introduction: WHY ISSA?

OR, I COULD TITLE THIS INTRODUCTION, "Why *Not* Bashō?" After all, Bashō is universally acclaimed as the seminal master of haiku, that one-breath poetic form that in his day as well as in Issa's went by the name of *haikai*. Issa himself acknowledged "old man" Bashō's precedence over the world of *haikai* and consciously sought to follow in his great predecessor's straw sandal-footsteps. As one Japanese critic, Nakamura Rikurō, pointed out in a 1921 study, the honorific moniker of "haiku master," while it applies so naturally and understandably to Bashō and, for that matter, to Buson; doesn't quite seem right for describing Issa (*Issa senshu* 4). One can easily imagine Bashō and Buson occupying seats of honor high over the heads of ordinary folk, but Issa seems to be one of us: standing alongside us, shoulder to shoulder. Bashō and Buson inspire reverence; Issa inspires love.

He was born in 1763 and grew up in the cold, misty highlands of Shinano Province, present-day Nagano Prefecture. His mother died when he was just a toddler, and he suffered in later childhood under the rule of his father's second, abusive wife. The theme of suffering clung to Issa his whole life: neglect, poverty, exile, ostracism, the deaths of his first four children, in childhood, and the death of his first wife, Kiku ("Chrysanthemum")—personal tragedies that are famously and forever associated with his name. Nevertheless, Issa's poetry isn't, as a rule, focused on doom and gloom. More typically, his haiku celebrate life on a living planet with appreciation, empathy, and good humor. Maybe this is why I and many of my fellow poets turn to Issa rather than to Bashō for our deepest inspirations. So human, so compassionate, so insightful; Issa has a lot to teach poets today, two centuries after.

To write like Issa means writing tenderly about one's fellow creatures, human and otherwise.

It means writing with an attitude of childlike perceptiveness, keeping one's mind and heart wide open to the universe and its infinite surprises.

It means writing with a willingness to laugh at life's intrinsic absurdities.

It means writing with bold subjectivity, defying all teachers and pundits who harp about the need for "objectivity" in haiku.

And, writing like Issa means writing with the kind of free-flowing imagination that discovers shockingly fresh juxtapositions and revelations.

This is not to deny that "Masters" Bashō and Buson at times exhibit many of these same qualities in their work. However, Issa writes consistently with such compassion, insight, humor, honesty, and leaping imagination, no one else, in my mind, is better qualified to teach by his example a Way of Haiku that is as alluring and as promising today in our twenty-first century as it once was in his late eighteenth, early nineteenth.

That's my belief. And maybe, after completing these lessons, you'll believe it too.

Let's find out . . .

Lesson 1. COMPASSION AS A WAY OF PERCEPTION, CONSCIOUSNESS, AND ART

KOBAYASHI ISSA, at least the Issa as self-portrayed in his poetry, had a big heart. He invited an orphan sparrow to play with him; he encouraged an outmatched, skinny frog to hang tough in a pond battle; he wondered aloud if his fleas too, in the long night, might be lonely.[1] Issa's concern for small, weak, alone, and oppressed creatures began with a genuine and sincere effort to imagine the world as experienced by them. He then affirmed his connection with fellow beings, acknowledging a shared reality in which he was not living on a higher plane looking down on them but, instead, was on their level, commiserating with them. From this effort of imagination joined to an awareness of connection and relationship, many haiku were born.

> morning cold—
> the toad's eyes too
> open wide[2]

> the lame chicken
> dragging, dragging . . .
> a long day[3]

Before commenting on these interesting verses, this caveat: all of the commentary about what a haiku might mean, in this book, is mine, only mine, and certainly incomplete. The wonderful capaciousness of haiku stems from that which is unspoken, leaving plenty of room for each reader's imagination and contemplation to fill in the gaps and make sense of it. So please regard whatever I say about haiku as simply one reader's always-provisional perception. Contemplate each verse on your own to conjure your own images, feelings, and ideas.

In the case of our first examples, my imagination and contemplation lead me to believe that Issa is intimately involved in these scenes. Although he says nothing directly about himself, his presence seems implicit. In the first haiku the word "too" (in Japanese, *mo*) provides a clue that *someone else* is experiencing the shock of cold temperature with eyes opened wide . . . in an expression of astonishment? Annoyance? Or, perhaps, could it be a wordless protest against a world that has suddenly grown cold: a winter world wherein life is symbolically (and for some creatures, literally) transitioning to death? The implied sharer in the scene *must* be Issa, I believe. He is the toad's peer and fellow traveler; he understands the toad's perplexity and, by commiserating and connecting with it, hints of his own.

As for the portrait of the lame chicken, Issa again seems to be fully present, in my reading of the haiku. The chicken has been limping for a long time now, implying that its observer has been noting this for a long time as well, a fact that might in itself suggest the observer's deep sympathy. One can imagine, between the lines, Issa's own feelings of stasis, boredom, and empathy for a disabled fellow creature. This isn't sappy sentimentality or childish anthropomorphism; it's simply a case of genuinely gaining insight into the experience of another living being. For a chicken too, the day is long; the suffering, also, is long. One can imagine that Issa, keenly aware of this suffering, suffers too.

Issa's first haiku lesson, the lesson of compassion, is actually a lesson in perception: a realization that other beings—even non-human ones—experience this same universe and, on some level, have feelings about those experiences. The connection to Buddhism is obvious. Issa believed (and often wrote) that animals were his cousins and friends from earlier lifetimes. It is quite natural for a Buddhist to honor the personhood of animals who, like human beings, might one day become Buddhas. However, one needn't be a Buddhist or Hindu or any type of believer in reincarnation to glean from Issa's animal poems valuable lessons in perception and feeling.

Perception and feeling are also paramount in this next example.

> the cricket's
> winter residence . . .
> my quilt[4]

Issa welcomes the cricket that has come to visit his bedding on a cold winter night as a roommate rather than as a pest. Again, it's a matter of perception. Issa acknowledges the life and sentience of his small visitor: the night is just as cold for a cricket as it is for a man. The world, for Issa, is a commonly shared space wherein a man and a cricket can enjoy a bed's comforting warmth on a winter's night. As usual with winter imagery in Issa's haiku, a notion of approaching death is hinted at, which serves to intensify the sense of the present moment's priceless value. Outside the walls of Issa's hut the universe is cold, vast, black, and unforgiving. Why *not* share this warmth, this moment of precious existence, with (even) a cricket?

Issa's compassion flows, we see in these haiku, from an authentic perception of *reality*, not from a fanciful make-believe world of "personified" toads, chickens, crickets . . . or flies.

> don't swat the fly!
> rubbing hands
> rubbing feet[5]

One's first impulse may be to swat, but Issa instead crouches for a close-up view of the fly, a view that he generously shares with his readers. The fly has tiny "hands" and "feet" rubbing together as if in supplication; as if, perhaps, it is praying. While at first the notion of a praying fly might seem the pinnacle of anthropomorphism, Issa's urgent plea to spare its life (directed at someone else or at himself?) can inspire a second, deeper look and consideration. Issa lived not only according to Buddhist principles; he also, like most Japanese people of his time, bowed and clapped his hands in prayer before the native gods of Shinto, the *kami-sama*. A key idea in Shinto is the indwelling divinity in natural things: animals, plants, mountains, rivers . . . From this ancient animistic perspective, even a fly carries a piece of God within it, and though the haiku is superficially humorous (we know that of *course* a fly can't "pray" in the human sense of the term), Issa's deeper message could well be that this fly's very existence honors God or the gods (depending on one's beliefs) and so to kill it for no important reason would be sinful. It would be a little sin, perhaps, but a sin nonetheless: the sin of failing to perceive the value of a life, however small.

Issa was not, we know from his journals, a vegetarian. Nevertheless, his references to killing animals in haiku hint of a deep concern.

> winter seclusion—
> cooking a chicken
> praising Buddha[6]

> evening moon—
> pond snails singing
> in the kettle[7]

The coldness of winter in the first example suggests the coldness of a world in which creatures that contain sparks of the divine either choose to or must kill and devour their fellow, divinely-infused creatures. The winter setting also suggests the coldness of the hearts of those who have forgotten (or never knew?) that all life is precious. Such people can cook a chicken as if it were a mere object, feeling neither remorse nor gratitude for a fellow being's sacrifice. And though the cook might fire off a quick prayer to Buddha, this attempt at self-exoneration seems feeble.

In the second example, the snails about to be eaten are "singing," which some readers interpret to be a reference to the hissing sound of steam escaping shells during the cooking process, though one optimistic Japanese friend of mine believes that the snails are merrily spitting water in a kettle that hasn't yet been heated. I lean toward the first, darker reading of the haiku, since Issa prefaces it with the head note, "Hell." Whether he is the cook, one of the diners who will enjoy the snails, or an onlooker; Issa's poem, set up by its prescript, indicates his appreciation of their predicament: they are trapped in an actual hell, burning in agony. Their "singing" might more accurately be translated as "crying."

Note that Issa has loaded these and all of our previous examples with emotions without relying on overtly emotional words. He lets his images speak for themselves, and they speak volumes. This is an important secret of great haiku.

Twenty-first century poets Deborah P Kolodji, Julie Warther, and Debbie Strange have learned this secret. They offer the following haiku as examples of verses imbued with Issa-like perspective and Issa-like compassion, their emotions encoded in pure imagery.

> one ant circles
> the toilet rim
> new roommate
> —Deborah P Kolodji

> heat of the day—
> the spider too
> in his hammock
> —Julie Warther

> first snow . . .
> three deer asleep
> in my garden
> —Debbie Strange

These poems are not parodies of Issa; they are original works of art for which the poets have adopted Issa's habits of mind. First, they stretched their imaginations to visualize what this world might look and feel like to fellow denizens of it: an ant, a spider, and three deer. Like Issa's warm quilts that he willingly shares with a cricket, a toilet rim is an intimate human space, yet an ant seems perfectly at home upon it, circling and exploring. Kolodji's christening of the ant as "roommate" reveals a feeling of connection and acceptance. There's no hint here of running for a can of insecticide.

Warner's spider in his "hammock," which dangles somewhere near the comparatively gargantuan one where the poet herself reclines, also must feel, she suggests, a contented coziness on this long summer day. The poet's ability to exercise her imagination to picture the experience of a spider in its web leads to an awareness of sameness and connection. Again, there's no rush to grab the Raid.

In the third example Strange suggests an abiding, shared sense of peace and security under the year's first snowflakes. The deer doze peacefully, while the poet, beyond mere tolerance of their presence, honors and celebrates it. The herbivores that she might chase off with a broom in warmer seasons adopt the poet's garden as their safe dormitory—and all is right with the world.

All three poets have learned Issa's lesson of imagining a fellow creature's perspective to the point that "it" and "I" become "we": sharing both space and consciousness. In addition, all three poets, like Issa, deftly allow their images alone to convey emotion. In the art of haiku, that which is unspoken often speaks the loudest.

If you are committed to actively reading this text, now would be a good time to set it aside, get out your writing equipment, close or open your eyes (whichever works for you), imagine or remember an encounter with a fellow creature, imagine its experience and perspective, and then, without announcing any emotions that you and it might be sharing in the moment (but definitely hinting of them), write a haiku. But first this note . . .

Whereas I and most haiku poets that I know began dabbling in haiku form by religiously adhering to the 5-7-5 syllable count advocated by our middle school teachers, you should feel free, if you like, to ignore syllable-counting completely—which, as you can see, Kolodji, Warther, and Strange most skillfully and effectively have done. The choice is yours.

Now, write.

***

In many poems Issa pushes his connection to nonhuman animals a step further, addressing them as if they are his peers who perfectly understand Japanese.

> O snail
> how do you make your living?
> autumn rain[8]
>
> evening lark—
> which pine island's
> good for sleeping?[9]

hey reed thrush
which way to ancient
Naniwa?[10]

heron on a post—
how is your year
ending?[11]

Certain hyper-serious critics have seized upon these and similar examples as proof that Issa is a mere "child's poet," unworthy of serious study. A major goal of my own criticism for the past twenty years has been to refute this trivialization of Issa. If we look at his haiku closely, we discover in most of them an underlying sense of respect for animal consciousness coupled with a conviction that the poet and the creature in question share many of the same challenges, perceptions, tendencies, and feelings. Such a vision, rooted in the ancient Asian spiritual traditions of Taoism, Shinto, and Buddhism, is not trivial, not a thing to scoff at or to dismiss as childish.

Issa acknowledges that a snail, too, must somehow make its living on a planet spinning through autumn toward winter (again hinting symbolically of approaching death). Issa and the snail experience the misery of cold rain drenching them on this shared planet. Issa also acknowledges that a lark has knowledge of the pine islands and that it, too, is a wanderer in this world. A reed thrush, as much as any human passerby, might indeed know the way to Naniwa, an ancient name for Okinawa, though whether it can communicate that knowledge to Issa is, of course, humorously suspect. And a heron on a post lives in the same seasonal reality on planet

Earth as people do. On some basic, perhaps instinctive level, they too respond to the ending of the year.

Issa didn't expect animals to answer him back, and I'm certain that he didn't expect them to understand his questions. Simply the fact that he acknowledged them as peers and fellow travelers on the planet in these and in hundreds of similar poems is an important, deep truth that followers of Issa must try to absorb.

Two centuries after Issa, Sue Colpitts addresses a fly in much the same spirit as he once addressed snails, larks, reed thrushes, and herons.

> relax, fly
> the spider and I
> are resting
> —Sue Colpitts

The fly runs no risk of being swatted by the poet or eaten by the spider . . . at least not in this present moment of languor, possibly a lazy summer afternoon, since "fly" is a summer season word in haiku. Colpitts triangulates three consciousnesses: her own, that of a resting spider, and that of a presumably restless, buzzing-about fly. Her deep perception into the moment makes her poem far more significant than a mere exercise in humor, though the fly's inability to understand or to respond does raise a smile. What *really* matters is the poet's consciousness of *its* consciousness, and the haiku's live-and-let-live message. Even a tiny, perhaps annoying, bundle of life has value.[12]

Issa's famous empathy also extends to his fellow human beings, especially to the poor and downtrodden.

> like the bats
> night's streetwalkers too
> make their slow rounds[13]
>
> the beggar child prays
> with trembling voice . . .
> for a doll[14]

Issa is a poet who refuses to depict himself as above or in any way superior to toads, chickens, crickets, flies, snails, larks, reed thrushes, or herons. It should come as no surprise, then, that he shows no sense of superiority over people who were considered by his contemporaries to be the dregs of early modern Japanese society: low-grade streetwalkers and beggars. As with his haiku about his interactions with animals, Issa wrote hundreds of haiku (like the above) in which he imagined the perspectives of downtrodden people with compassion and insight. He imagined himself into the minds of streetwalkers (*yahochi*: "night hawks") who, like bats or the birds of the night after which they are named, eked out a living in the shadows. And he imagined himself into the mind of a beggar child who, on the day of the annual Doll Festival (Third Month, third day) asks the gods and, indirectly, her parents, for something that cannot be provided. Issa portrays in a breath the sadness of a little girl and the breaking hearts of her parents.

Alain Kervern, a contemporary Breton poet, shares Issa's ability to imaginatively penetrate the psyche of sufferers, disclosing their pain through images alone.

> it's not the rain
> someone crying tonight
> on the stairs[15]
> —Alain Kervern

> neighborhood festival
> she puts on makeup tonight
> to hide the bruises[16]
> —Alain Kervern

In the first haiku we don't know who is weeping or why; we only know that the sound of it mingles confusedly with that of the night downpour. The scene presents two people in both a physical and metaphorical darkness: one person crying and one listening, but there is no connection between them revealed in the poem other than the fact that one is hearing the other. Each of them seems profoundly alone in the night, despite the fact that they exist under the same roof, under the same rain.

The second haiku, about a neighborhood festival, also is set at night and also implies darkness beyond the physical. The woman hides bruises that she will not expose to her community. She literally paints on a face to attend the celebration, keeping the abuse that she is suffering hidden deep in the shadows of her domicile and her mind.

It's not easy to suggest empathy for fellow beings through poetic image alone, but Kervern does this masterfully—as do American poet J. Zimmerman, Bulgarian poet Ludmila Balabanova, and Colombian poet Victoria Eugenia Gómez M. If poverty and homelessness sadly circle the globe, so do haiku of compassion in the style of Issa.

> sky of stars
> above the trashcan fire
> dirt-streaked faces
> —J. Zimmerman

> No coins—
> I dropped in the beggar's hat
> a sigh[17]
> —Ludmila Balabanova

> without coins the girl
> her best smile
> for the beggar[18]
> —Victoria Eugenia Gómez M.

These are all poems of open-eyed, open-hearted awareness. Issa, who wrote scores of haiku about beggars and poor people, would approve of them, I think.

> in the box
> four or five *mon* . . .
> night of winter rain[19]

Issa isn't heavy-handed or preachy in his haiku

portraits of poverty. To write like him means learning how to commiserate *light*-handedly (if that's a word). In Issa's time four or five *mon* (a coin) could almost, but not quite, pay for a small bowl of rice. By focusing his attention (and the reader's) on this paltry sum inside a box under a cold nocturnal rain, the poet speaks volumes about the reality of the unmentioned beggar. In the art of haiku, as mentioned earlier, less is more. Issa focuses on so little here—just a few coins in a box in a rain—and yet he manages to lay bare a poor person's entire universe, including a society that not only tolerates his or her poverty and destitution but, in its very structure, has possibly required it. The rain falling in and on such a world is cold, indeed.

Petar Tchouhov—a Bulgarian poet, novelist, songwriter, singer, guitarist, and band leader—evokes similar emotional depth with similar deft minimalism. Perfectly bilingual, Tchouhov composed the following haiku in English.

> night storm
> I'm thinking about
> the dolls in the attic
> —Petar Tchouhov

The verse reminds me a lot of Kervern's one about the mysterious weeper on the stairs; something about rain at night in all of these poems by Kervern, Tchouhov, and Issa establishes a feeling of profound existential loneliness in a vast, indifferent universe. Tchouhov's master stroke is to reach out emotionally not to a fellow human being but, surprisingly, to dolls: human simulacra that, confined in the attic, might symbolically represent a forever lost, locked up, and shut away childhood. To write like Issa—that is, with an open, sympathetic heart—doesn't mean being sappy or maudlin. Tchouhov's terse little poem is great precisely because it hints without explaining, leaving ample space for readers to ponder, imagine, and feel.

In some poems Issa's compassion for the poor and suffering seems so great that one detects an undertone of condemnation of the cruel status quo.

> the bill collector
> with shoes on steps inside
> the hearth[20]

A bill collector is never a welcome visitor, but on this particular cold winter's day, he steps rudely into a house without removing his shoes, ignoring Japanese etiquette and hurrying to warm himself at the hearth. The poem expresses empathy for the implied poor person in the scene (possibly Issa), who is about to become poorer. It also expresses a sense of quiet outrage at an injustice.

Issa introduces this next poem in his journal with the prose note, "feeling pity for a widow alone in the world."

> when your village is done
> where next?
> rice-planting umbrella-hat[21]

After planting rice in her own village, the widow will travel to another one, and perhaps to many others after that, to perform the same back-breaking toil. In Issa's day the transplantation of rice stalks into flooded fields was hard labor performed to the relentless rhythm of communal rice-planting songs. Issa shines a bright light on the monotonous and difficult lives of this woman and her fellow rice-growing peasants upon whom the wealth of the nation depended. His simple question, "where next?" is filled with sympathy for her with a hint of sadness about the social reality in which she found herself trapped.

Some poets today carry on Issa's project of exposing suffering and inequality. In the twenty-first century, however, the call for social change perhaps sounds louder in haiku than Issa could have dared to attempt in shogun-controlled Tokugawa Japan. For example, Elliot Nicely's little poem about sparrows isn't *just* about sparrows.

> in the crook
> of the no vacancy sign
> cold sparrows
>   —Elliot Nicely

Sparrows huddle together for warmth, but since the "no vacancy" message is meant for people to read, Nicely suggests that there might also be people out in the cold who will remain in the cold, shelterless. Cold night, cold world, cold hearts . . .

Marietta Jane McGregor and Lynn Halley Allgood also create poetic scenes wherein the reality of animals and human beings coincides.

> chewed power bill
> the mice and I
> all feel cold
> —Marietta Jane McGregor

> hornet's nest
> on the porch
> eviction notice
> —Lynn Halley Allgood

In a modern society, people without adequate funds (or adequate credit) can find themselves shivering on cold nights, if unable to pay the power bill, and can find themselves homeless, if unable to pay the rent. These poems by McGregor and Allgood resonate with deep feeling while hinting that the human world, as currently organized, is neither fair nor right.

A haiku by Rick Clark, superficially about a butterfly, also resonates with timely social and political implications.

> border crossing—
> a cabbage butterfly flits
> from daisy to daisy
> —Rick Clark

The butterfly can fly freely, blissfully unconscious of the human construct of a border. Without breathing a word about the injustice of a rich nation (founded by immigrants) slamming shut its iron door to the poor, the destitute, and the politically oppressed of other lands; Clark implies all this. The butterfly seeks daisies, and people at the border seek a better life, but the latter are stopped. Issa wrote a similar haiku about a prison.

> in and out
> of prison it goes . . .
> baby sparrow[22]

Someone travels freely in and out of a prison, but we must wait until Issa's punch line to discover the identity of that someone: a baby sparrow! It flies easily and innocently back and forth between the carefully demarcated human realms of "prison" and "freedom." Such categories, of course, mean nothing to it. In their poems, Clark and Issa challenge readers to contemplate the suffering that borders and prisons can cause. Though neither haiku is overtly political, both call for a revolution of the imagination, coaxing readers to imagine and feel deeply the suffering of fellow human beings: rejected immigrants, unseen prisoners. Such empathy is perhaps a necessary prerequisite for genuine change.

Write like Issa. Write with compassion yet

understatement. Leave space for your readers' minds to wander and wonder.

But before you do, here are a few additional and, I hope, inspiring examples of twenty-first century poets whose haiku exude compassion for fellow animals, fellow people, and even for "fellow" trees and weeds.

> first short-sleeve day
> the midges also welcome
> spring
> —Autumn Noelle Hall

> I'm sorry, I'm so sorry
> the small spider crushed
> under my fear
> —Cyndi Lloyd

> where to house
> 50 million souls
> turkey heaven
> —Robert Epstein

> not easily brushed off
> I offer the tick
> a drink
> —Julie Warther

> all day I watch
> that one-winged crow
> summer sky
> —Dyana Basist

sunset mountain—
don't worry, mosquitoes,
I can walk alone!
    —David Rachlin

I'm sorry
for the dead dog
not the flies
    —Marietta Jane McGregor

cricket
your song woos
only the sun
    —Victor Ortiz

you can't say
our paths crossed!
the mouse's eyes
    —Tom Sacramona

arthritis
a hot-water bottle
for the catbed
    —Mary Stevens

cold morning
two stray cats
in the doghouse
    —Petar Tchouhov

sunset
the hare and I
stop to watch
    —Anna Maris

Buddhist monk
hesitates . . . then steps
on a wasp
   —Nika

a "Lost Dog" sign
nailed deep
into the oak
   —David G. Lanoue

my scythe
I spare those
with flowers
   —Robert Henry Poulin

Lesson 2. CHILDLIKE VISION: THE JOY AND NECESSITY OF UNLEARNING

> baby sparrows
> move aside!
> Sir Horse passes[23]

ISSA, as mentioned earlier, is sometimes wrongly pigeonholed as a "child's poet," a provider of delight for Japanese preschoolers who happily memorize and proudly recite some of his famous verses, like the one in which he warns baby sparrows to beware the hooves of Sir Horse. When they grow older, however, they usually read no further into Issa's vast canon of over twenty thousand poems. He thus becomes forever associated in their minds with childhood and the things of childhood to be left behind when they grow up: a sad distortion of a serious haiku master's lifelong work. As we noted in Lesson 1, Issa in fact wrote many perceptive poems that plumb the depths of his fellow creature's lives and suffering. Since compassion is a core value of Buddhism, Issa's poetry of insight into other beings reveals his spiritual maturity, not childishness. Relegating him to the colorful bookshelves of kindergartens is simply unfair.

There's another reason that many of Issa's Japanese readers over the course of two centuries have appreciated his haiku mainly as children's literature. Like no other haiku poet, Issa chats with babies and small children in his one-breath verses, describes them minutely, and participates fully in their joy and pain. Just as he imaginatively penetrates the realities of snails and frogs, Issa stoops low to see children eye-to-eye and, more importantly, to see the surrounding world as they see it. Perceiving this planet's shimmering green grass and dazzling blue sky with the eyes of a child turns out to be an exceedingly grownup aesthetic practice grounded in ancient spiritual traditions of Asia: the Taoism of Laozi (Lao Tzu) that advocates adopting the perspective of infants, and the pure-hearted Pure Land Buddhism of Shinran for whom the pinnacle of devotion is a state of non-calculating, childlike trust.

I have written elsewhere about how Issa's poetic consciousness requires the perhaps impossible-sounding exercise of becoming a child again, so I won't repeat all of that argument here.[24] I'll just mention two key points. First, if one regards childhood as a mode of consciousness rather than as a state rigidly defined by chronological age, thinking and perceiving as a child is a real possibility for adults. Secondly, the idea of returning to childlike consciousness is supported by recent work in neurology involving the "Default-Mode Network" (DMN), a brain region that develops as one matures, replacing the primary consciousness of infancy.[25] The DMN is the adult's sense of awareness that screens out the bulk of sensory experience so that colors once perceived intensely by a child grow duller over time: no more shimmering grass, no more dazzling sky . . . just "green" here and "blue" there, barely noticed by an adult mind preoccupied with plans that keep it focused on the future and consequently (tragic for a haiku poet) out of touch with the present moment.

Laozi's ancient advice to return to a state of infancy, along with his insistence that wisdom requires daily *un*learning, aligns perfectly with a contemporary scientific view of the human brain.[26] It is possible, whether assisted by meditation or by psychedelic drugs, to at least momentarily exit adult consciousness and re-enter the primordial awareness of early childhood. "Unlearning" involves the setting aside of grownup prejudices, assumptions, and black-and-white definitions: plunging one's self wholly into the here-and-now moment to experience life without the adult brain's filters and blinders.

To write like Issa, we first need to think like Issa, which means opening ourselves to now-moments (which may include also remembered and imagined moments) without preconceptions. Childlike openness enables one to experience ordinary moments of life on Earth as they truly are: wondrous. For example, when cows come lowing in a thick spring mist, their sound seems as palpable as their ponderous, slowly materializing bodies.

> moo, moo, moo
> from the mist cows
> emerge[27]

Issa understood that the most ordinary things can seem like astounding revelations if we remain open-minded and open-hearted, drinking in the world's colors, textures, and sounds with our perhaps long-neglected child-consciousness that our adult sense of self (the DMN) has supplanted but not destroyed. Nicholas M. Sola appears to understand this too.

> spring forest—
> all the colors
> of socks
> —Nicholas M. Sola

I hope that Sola will accept it as a high compliment when I describe his perception in this haiku as childlike. Achieving childlike vision as he manages to do here is actually quite a difficult task, analogous to Pablo Picasso's artistic evolution from "grownup" realism to colorful and whimsical creations that sing of his inner child set free. The adult mind compartmentalizes: forests and socks occupy distinct and separate realms of experience in such a mind. The child's mind, however, combines and blurs: so many colors in these woods, so many socks! The connection isn't logical (the purview of adult thinking) but magical. Sola opens himself to wonder and to magic, here and now, and a marvelous haiku results.

When I solicited submissions of Issa-like haiku for this book, by far the highest number of poems received had to do with compassion, the theme of Lesson 1, which is hardly surprising, given Issa's famous tenderness toward fellow creatures, human and otherwise. Far fewer haiku received exhibited our theme for the present lesson, childlike vision, a fact that illustrates the high degree of difficulty for adults to perceive and write in this manner. One way to get started on the process of exiting one's adult mode of thinking and perception, akin to obeying a hypnotist's command for one to stare closely and intently at a swinging pendulum or some fixed spot in space, is to gaze patiently at something small, keeping your mind open and ready for amazement.

> tiny green beetle
> a mirror on her back
> crossing my arm
> —Kath Abela Wilson

> slight tilt of the earth
> a spider drinking
> the dew
> —Meik Blöttenberger

Without embellishments Wilson and Blöttenberger present extreme close-up visions of nature, reminding us of the experience that one has when peering through a microscope. The universe, so ordinary and so easy to ignore by adult minds, suddenly appears weird and wonderful under magnification. In truth, the universe *is* weird and wonderful, but our grownup brains have screened out and have forgotten this fact. A return to a childlike apprehension of the world's beetles and spiders means a return to a more authentic experience of reality.

Another truth forgotten by most people after childhood is a feeling of seamless connection with all that surrounds them. Adult thinking, in contrast, emphasizes one's separateness from everything else. Reviving child-consciousness means returning to a feeling of inseparableness from the universe, which is not only a step toward good haiku but, in a spiritual sense, a step toward enlightenment.

> stars in the night sky
> appears to be salt
> sprinkling on me
> —Steve Greene

Greene guilelessly perceives stars as salt much as a child might do, and in a moment of childlike perceptual magic, he senses the sparkling cosmos sprinkling down over his body: a celebration of innocent, pure connection that adult thinking could never produce.[28]

Robert Epstein writes a haiku with similar innocence of perspective and thought.

> baby calf
> baby lamb
> baby jesus
> —Robert Epstein

This is not poetry of adult consciousness even though an adult wrote it. Epstein dares, as Issa did, to embrace the simplicity and sincerity of childlike vision, and in doing so he makes a startling statement about the sacredness of life and the cruelty of human beings. He begins with two baby animals commonly served on dinner plates, but then, surprisingly, includes in their number, in the same breath, "baby jesus." The poem is childlike in its vision and simple in its form but deeply insightful, inviting readers to consider the murder of a sacrificial "Lamb of God" on a cross in juxtaposition with the slaughter of young, innocent, and (literally) tender creatures.

Tom Sacramona focuses his poetic attention on a different baby animal.

> a puppy
> licking the dew
> off everything
> —Tom Sacramona

The haiku's last word and image, "everything," is a charming, perhaps naïve-sounding exaggeration, but if we as readers follow the puppy's busy tongue in our imaginations, we might also explore a world turned fresh and new at dawn, a universe of infinite surprises and delights: the living, green world in which we once reveled before adult consciousness banished us from that Eden. In a similarly attentive, non-cerebral haiku Issa might be describing the same puppy later that same day, exhausted from its explorations.

> the sleeping puppy
> paws
> at the willow[29]

In my online archive note for this haiku, I wrote, "There's no deep level of meaning, no hidden symbolism, yet this simple image is powerful—oozing with love." Indeed, the poem could have served as a good example in our first lesson about writing with compassion, since Issa's warm feeling for the puppy is obvious. However, this image of a sleeping puppy pawing at drooping green leaves also exemplifies childlike perception and consciousness. Issa's puppy, like Sacramona's, is happily immersed in nature. Both poets, in their visions of these puppies, are likewise immersed in it with accepting, non-defining, and non-limiting awareness. Their minds are simply *open.*

John Hawkhead achieves similar perception and consciousness in a haiku about an older animal.

> the old black cat
> still chasing snowflakes
> on tiptoes
> —John Hawkhead

The image isn't contrived; the haiku isn't an intellectual exercise. Instead, Hawkhead sets aside— that is, he *un*learns—grownup notions about what is worth paying attention to, along with grownup ideas about poetry, particularly the expectation that poets are important people who spout important ideas in order to show off their importance. Instead, he gazes innocently and deeply, discovering a still curious, playful kitten inside the body of an old cat. In a sense, the old black cat and the observing poet are twin souls: the cat manages to recover, if only for a brief moment, the irrepressible energy of its long-past kittenhood. And the poet recovers, in this moment, the primordial consciousness of his earliest years. The cat dances lightly on tiptoes; Hawkhead's heart, as he perceives and shares the scene, dances too.

Issa's simplicity is deceptive. Some readers misconstrue it to mean shallowness of feeling and idea, but nothing could be farther from the truth. Contemporary haiku poets who consider themselves "avant-garde"—or, to use the Japanese term, *gendai* artists—have begun a disturbing trend of re-defining haiku to mean short, obtuse, experimental language games that only seem to proclaim the poet's cleverness for cleverness's sake. Issa's example of two centuries ago is needed now more than it ever was, to lead poets away from the self-important and self-aggrandizing adult mind and toward the open, selfless consciousness of early childhood.

> trying to pinch
> a bead of dew . . .
> a child[30]

> garden butterfly—
> the child crawls, it flies
> crawls, it flies[31]

These haiku by Issa are not only *about* children; they exemplify childlike perception: remaining open to, entranced by, and forever curious about this universe's glittering dewdrops and bright, flitting butterflies.

Marcyn Del Clements and Rick Tarquinio reveal their own openness and curiosity about this wondrous, odd world in which they, too, find themselves immersed.

> in mangroves
> looking for moon jellies
> by starlight
>   —Marcyn Del Clements

> after the storm
> soaking wet horses
> shaking off flies
> —Rick Tarquinio

There is no clever language play here, no obscure chain of abstract reasoning. And if certain avant-garde poets in Japan and around the world might disdain the purity and simplicity of Del Clements' and Tarquinio's poems of deeply felt, wide-eyed experience; let them. They simply don't know, and probably will never know, what they are missing.

Issa subscribed to a poetic art that emerges from genuine, immersive encounters with the universe, and that leads readers to imaginatively plunge into those moments themselves.

> dogs sparkling
> with fireflies
> sound asleep[32]

> hailstones—
> look! there's one behind
> brother's ear[33]

With disarming openness Issa drinks in his discoveries and records them on the page. Dogs are unaware of the glittering constellations of fireflies decorating them in the night, but Issa sees, marvels, and writes. Or perhaps, in truth, Issa remembers or imagines the scene, since we know from his journals that he often wrote about springtime in the dead of winter, and about Edo while sitting in his home deep in the Shinano mountains, hundreds of kilometers away. What matters is that the origin of Issa's poetry lies always in real experience of this world's dogs, fireflies, hailstones, and everything else. These experiences can later be remembered or even imaginatively altered in the composition of haiku, but the resulting poem, to repeat, arises from *real* experience (more on this in Lesson 5).

To write like Issa means writing perceptively with minimum interference from the adult brain's self-censorship, self-criticism, self-importance, second-guessing, and poetry-killing notions of what poetry is, particularly haiku poetry. It means daring to see, imagine, and sound like a child, because, after all, "out of the mouths of babes oft times come gems."

One such gem is this remarkable haiku by Marian Olson.

> laughing,
> kids in the yard mimic
> the headless hen
>   —Marian Olson

The meaning of the laughter in the scene depends on how old the reader wishes to imagine these "kids." Very young tots might be laughing with innocent glee as they whirl about the yard, imitating the hen's wild last dance. Older children, who somewhat grasp the finality of death, might be laughing with savagery and perhaps even with an edge of guilt-drowning hysteria. Olson challenges the reader to decide: Are the children tiny and oblivious to the cruelty of the grownup world, or are they a bit older and finding themselves being initiated into this cruelty? One might even choose to picture in the scene an emotionally complex mingling of children's ages. Olson's haiku is a one-breath treatise on neurological and social development, coaxing readers to contemplate how the innocence of children's early minds is gradually supplanted by an ego that stresses their separation from nature, that posits "us" versus "them," winners versus losers, people who matter and animals that don't.

Robert Witmer also strikes deep into truth in a poem about potted plants.

> summer rain . . .
> potted plants
> push against the glass
> —Robert Witmer

At first glance, the haiku seems innocently anthropomorphic, positing that indoor plants, thirsty for the rain, are pushing against the glass of a window as if longing to go outside and be drenched. Upon further reflection, the poem suggests a deeper message: the plants are captives that have been forcibly removed from the wild. The glass between them and the rain represents a see-through prison wall. The haiku, though eminently simply, works also as a parable on human existence. Like the potted plants, something inside us longs for contact with the summer rain, but most of us never follow this healthy impulse of our inner child. We remain indoors, keeping panes of glass between us and an immersive return to nature and to childlike awareness.

One Christmas vacation, I was visiting my elderly parents in Omaha, Nebraska. An experience that I had in the middle of the night led to this haiku.

> someone else
> couldn't sleep, the warm
> toilet seat
> —David G. Lanoue

In the moment I felt the warm "touch" of a fellow human being through my bottom. But in that moment I also felt how dark the house was, how deep my sense of loneliness. Whether it was my mother or my father who had sat on the toilet before me, I didn't know. I felt somehow close to that unknown person, yet also incredibly, sadly distant. A simple experiential encounter with unexpected warmth in a bathroom in a house in the frozen Omaha suburbs led to the haiku, which in turn led me to reflect on the presence and absence of loved ones: of touch but also of not touching. This experience-based poem, which exists only because I followed Issa's example of simply accepting any and all experiences as worthy of attention and suitable for haiku, made me think (and *still* makes me think) about how very alone we are in this world, we children in the darkness.

I close this lesson with five more examples of childlike vision in haiku. After looking them over, please feel free to write your own. Reflect on a past or present experience without your adult blinders, and write that experience into a one-breath poem. Don't be afraid if your haiku doesn't sound fancy or important—for this is actually a good thing. Invite your inner child to simply "Come out, come out, wherever you are!"

the silent party
after the guests leave
ant covered shrimp
   —Kath Abela Wilson

plum blossom
in and out of buddha's shadow
a pair of squirrels
   —Angelee Deodhar

wildflowers . . .
great are the affairs
of bees
   —Julie Warther

Independence Day—
the carpenter ants march
in their own parade
   —P. M. Issa

birch felled
woodpile at the wall
splinter in my thumb[34]
   —Traude Veran

Lesson 3. COMIC VISION, COSMIC JOKES

IN THE PREVIOUS LESSON we looked at how Issa opened his mind to a vibrant universe of sensations without adult filters or preconceptions, and we tried to do this as well. In this lesson, his trademark humor becomes our focus, which may at first seem a completely different and separate thing, but really it isn't. In fact, Issa's haiku humor arises quite naturally and perhaps inevitably from his childlike, non-judging and non-censoring consciousness.

> spring breeze—
> the great courtier
> poops in the field[35]
>
> pooping in the field—
> avert your eyes
> little wren![36]

Many adults might not consider defecation to be a proper subject for poetry, but Issa's less grownup, less rigid mind opens wide to, and revels in, instances of potty humor. Both of these poems about outdoor pooping were composed in 1814 (the first in Seventh Month, the second in Tenth Month), but Issa wrote many similar haiku on this subject over the years. Ten years earlier, for example, he portrayed in a memorable haiku a high priest of a Buddhist temple performing this same important bodily function in a field while a poor acolyte held a parasol over his superior's head. These poems find comedy in incongruities: the incongruity of socially important officials performing a humbling but necessary biological task; the incongruity of imputing an understanding of human etiquette and modesty to a bird. The childlike consciousness explored in the previous lesson serves as a necessary precondition for such poetic jokes to arrive on the page.

Many of Issa's haiku indeed are structured and function like jokes. They begin with a setup—such as, "spring breeze / the great courtier . . ."—followed by a punch line: "poops in the field." Using a bait-and-switch tactic, he leads readers to expect one thing—in the case of a great courtier, some sort of dignified action—and then he switches suddenly to the unexpected: the important courtier is . . . *pooping!* Or, as in the second example, Issa begins with an intrinsically incongruous image ("pooping in the field")—incongruous in itself because it conflicts with the norm for worthy subjects for poetry—and then, in his punch line, adds a second incongruity: the notion that a wren should modestly look away.

Although such verses are shaped and work like jokes, this is not to say that they are *only* jokes. In fact, they are fine haiku capable of conveying profound feeling and meaning. The image of a great courtier responding to nature's call, for example, invites readers literally to peek under the robe of authority and glimpse the naked animal beneath. They may laugh, but they also may meditate on the implications of this stripping away of social hierarchy. And when Issa tells a wren to avert its eyes, the joke's deeper resonance reminds readers that even a tiny bird is worthy of concern. Though it's absurd to think that a wren has human prudishness, the implication that it deserves notice, address, respect, and love is a serious idea for Issa, perhaps his most important theme in a lifetime of writing.

Readers familiar with the various genres of Japanese poetry might be asking: Aren't these humorous poems by Issa in fact examples of senryu, not haiku? On its surface, a Japanese senryu looks exactly like a haiku, with seventeen syllables and a hard break or "cut" that divides the poem (usually) into two phrases of either five and twelve syllables or twelve and five. Its tone is highly satirical, and for subject matter focuses on human foibles. Although many of Issa's verses are indeed humorous and poke fun at human shortcomings, Issa didn't label them as senryu. Instead, he consistently referred to his poetry as *haikai* (what today we call haiku), which suggests that he didn't think of his comic poems as exercises in shallow mockery. As we have seen in the above-cited poems about public pooping, even Issa's funniest verses can achieve great emotional and symbolic depth, giving readers not only smiles and chuckles but also food for thought.

Issa's comic vision presents surprises and odd discoveries that utterly function as haiku.

> baby grass—
> the stylish woman leaves
> her butt print[37]

> on the tip
> of Buddha's nose . . .
> a fart bug[38]

> a farting contest –
> harvest moon night
> in the hut[39]

In the first example the new grass is tender and green; the woman, we can imagine, is young, attracttive, elaborately coiffed, and wrapped in a brightly patterned kimono of the latest style. The two images exude freshness and beauty, but surprisingly, when the pretty lady rises from where she has been sitting, she leaves an imprint of crushed grass. The "delicate" woman reveals herself to be, in fact, a gargantuan smasher of grass blades, viewed from the grass's perspective (which, of course, compassionate Issa adopts). The derrière trace that she leaves "behind" is both accusatory—reminding readers of the Buddhist dictum to value all life, however small—and funny.

In the second example a Japanese stink bug—literally, a "fart bug"—sits on the tip of a stone or wooden Buddha's nose. Again Issa discovers incongruity in the scene: the serene epitome of enlightenment shares center stage with a stinky insect, bringing together in one breath lofty and low, important and insignificant, spiritual and loathsome. The fact that the fart bug perches on the Buddha's nose suggests that the Awakened One cannot look away, cannot ignore it. It's as if the bug is demanding the Buddha's (and our) full attention, telling him (and us): "Look at me! I'm part of this universe too!" While we may laugh, we also realize, deep down, that the fart bugs of this world are, indeed, just as essential as its Buddhas.

The third example again mentions farting—an

intrinsically funny phenomenon since, as an involuntary bodily event, it subverts pretenses of human self-control and dignity. Here again, Issa discovers, in a moment of childlike, accepting consciousness, a shocking juxtaposition: the resplendent and (according to Shinto) sacred harvest moon shines over a farting contest below: the sublime joined with the worldly, the serious with the silly. The joke, again, is a cosmic joke being played by the universe itself and only reported by Issa. This world is a place of ethereal beauty; this world is a place of farts.

Stanford M. Forrester and Alan Summers follow Issa's lead in their haiku about cats. In both of these examples, the poets function more like discoverers than inventors; they open their senses and minds to, and enjoy the rewards of, punch lines courtesy of the universe.

> dinner time—
> the old cat regains
> his hearing
> —Stanford M. Forrester

> open window
> the cat dozes
> half in half out
> —Alan Summers

Petar Tchouhov and James Won make similar discoveries about the world of people.

> shooting gallery
> the hunter wins
> a teddy bear
> —Petar Tchouhov

> a fix on fitness
> once outside the gym
> she lights up
> —James Won

Issa's haiku humor is, most often, found humor. Poets who follow his lead find their own revelations of odd concatenations: a "deaf" cat that miraculously hears the call to dinner, a cat sprawling and dozing both inside and outside a house, a hunter substituting a toy gun for his rifle to bag a stuffed bear, and a gym rat, after working out for the sake of her physical health, lighting up a cancer stick.

Many readers associate Issa with tragedy, remembering the deaths of his mother, grandmother, father, four children, and first wife—and recalling the heartbroken haiku that he wrote to deal with all of these personal horrors. One Japanese critic even went so far as to title a book about Issa, "The Sorrows of Human Life."[40] This view of the poet, though common, is distorted. If we consider his poetry in its entirety—well over twenty thousand one-breath verses—we find that he is more often a poet of comic rather than tragic vision. Tragedy, in a Buddhist understanding, grows out of one's attachment to the ephemeral things of this world, particularly attachment to people who, of course, inevitably die. The tragic gesture is one of clinging. The comic gesture, in contrast, grows from an enlightened Buddhist perspective. Instead of clinging to things of a universe in a state of flux, one opens one's hands, gives up, lets go . . . and laughs. This is an insightful spiritual attitude embodied in familiar Asian statues of a paunchy Laughing Buddha.

> pointing
> at the fart bug . . .
> laughing Buddha[41]

In this wonderfully quirky haiku by Issa the Buddha points at, and calls attention to, the living incongruity of a fart bug . . . and laughs. The Buddha invites us to do the same—or, I should say, Issa, by creating this poetic image, issues an invitation for us to choose the liberating comic gesture of laughter and acceptance in our own lives.

Sometimes Issa finds humor in the biologically serious matter of sex.

> while I'm away
> enjoy your lovemaking
> hut's flies[42]

On the surface it seems silly to imply that the flies of the hut, as if possessing human modesty (like the earlier-mentioned wren), would wait for the poet to go away before commencing their orgy. On a deeper level, however—a level that Issa's jokes usually only barely hide—the poem suggests that even tiny flies enjoy the sensation of pleasure. Issa's joke reveals a deep existential truth.

> winter morning
> the only ones having sex
> are banana slugs
>   —Dyana Basist

love
on a thin wire—
two pigeons[43]
    —Ludmila Balabanova

just born from the lake
and already having sex—
bug hatch
    —Rick Clark

fast and furious
we mate
like dragonflies
    —Kath Abela Wilson

Like Issa, Basist, Balabanova, Clark, and Wilson focus poetically on copulation and discover humor therein. Basist's banana slugs engaging in slimy sex are "the only ones" doing this, hinting that she is among the many creatures on this cold morning without a lover's embrace. Feeling jealous of the love life of slugs is weirdly funny, but perhaps, upon deeper reflection, touching and melancholic.

    Balabanova portrays an awkward and precarious balancing act. Her two pigeons are determined daredevils, especially the male who mounts the female without regard to their mutual safety. His singleminded horniness makes him a comic figure, a stereotype of male lust. Balabanova invites her readers to think about the ridiculous moves and risks undertaken by the males of many species, including those of *homo sapiens*, when seeking (in Mick Jagger's sense of the word) satisfaction.

    Rick Clark presents the visual joke of babies

having babies, but within its humor one of life's deepest mysteries reveals itself. Significantly, the bugs have been newly hatched from the lake, water being an archetypal mother symbol. Without bothering with stages of childhood or adolescence, they plunge right into the urgent business of procreation. Clark's humorous haiku lays bare a truth about life on planet Earth. Life is sex; sex is life.

Kath Abela Wilson compares her own lovemaking to the quick encounter of two dragonflies. She lets the reader decide on the haiku's tone. Is she dissatisfied with the hasty sex act, or might she be proud of behaving so naturally and carnally, like the "fast and furious" insects? And might she be alluding to the over-the-top, adrenaline-drenched *Fast and Furious* action movie franchise, thus caricaturing and making fun of her own bedroom escapades? The poem raises big smiles and big questions.

We've already noted Issa's potty humor. William Scott Galasso follows his example. Like Issa, Galasso dares simply to open his senses to a moment, to feel, and to record.

> father and son
> laughing as the snow
> turns yellow
> —William Scott Galasso

Leaving adult propriety behind, Galasso happily returns us to a more innocent time of life where children (especially boys) find delight in outdoor piddling. This yellowing of snow not only celebrates an intimate connection of warm bodies with the vast winter world of nature; for the father and son it provides an occasion for wordless, side-by-side bonding. Their natural response to such naughty fun (*especially* fun, if they happen to be city folk), is irrepressible laughter.

Also writing like Issa, humorously and with deep resonance, is Elliot Nicely.

> constipated—
> the long echo
> of a train's horn
> —Elliot Nicely

This haiku could easily serve as an example in our fifth lesson, dedicated to Issa's flexible imagination that enables unexpected leaps of association from one image to another. However, its built-in humor is so striking, I feel that it belongs here. Constipation certainly ranks far below cherry blossoms and harvest moons on a list of the most common topics for haiku. In fact, since this is the *only* constipation haiku that I'm aware of, I would dare say that it ranks at or near the very bottom of such a list. This is one source of the poem's humor: its opening image constitutes such a jarring surprise in relation to ordinary topics of haiku poetry. From this initial surprise, Nicely shifts (nicely) to a second surprise: the sound of "the long echo/ of a train's horn." Nicely leaves plenty of space for the reader's imagination to work. I choose to picture the poor, constipated subject of the poem up late at night in a bathroom, straining without success until, instead of physical relief, the only "blast" in the night is that of the distant horn. Other readers—including the poet, I suspect—will conjure different details, but the basic elements of the scene—constipation and a faraway train horn—tell a mournful tale of frustration and loneliness that is so human . . . and so funny.

It has been several weeks since I first read Nicely's haiku, yet still it continues to pop into my mind from time to time, as if inviting me to muse over its deeper implications. Re-reading and re-imagining it now, I reflect on associations with the word "constipated" that didn't occur to me initially. I think, for example, about writer's block and, more generally, those times that a person feels the internal pressure of half-formed plans and dreams trapped inside, unable to emerge. The constipated person listening to a train horn's lonely echo now expands in significance for me to stand for all artists or even, in a sense, for all human beings. The urge to create builds up inside us, and the inability to bring that urge to fruition causes real agony. This is plainly not a senryu but a great haiku with great emotional and symbolic depth.

A successful comic haiku in the style of Issa should provoke, in a breath, both laughter and thought.

> bent christmas tree
> more tinsel in my hair
> this year
> —Autumn Noelle Hall

Autumn Noelle Hall writes on a theme that Issa himself felt drawn to repeatedly: the aging process. Like Issa, she finds humor in this unavoidable fact of life.

> New Year's tooth-hardening
> meal . . . the cat wins
> and laughs[44]

In New Year's season a special tooth-hardening meal is served, but Issa, who writes often and nostalgically about his lost teeth, alludes to the futility of his own partaking of it. The cat, which we can imagine has a full, healthy set, is laughing at him, Issa imagines. In Hall's haiku the old Christmas tree (evidently an artificial one), now "bent" with age, leans in such a way that more of its tinsel gets tangled in her hair. The silver tinsel suggests, in turn, silver hair—of which the poet may indeed have more "this year." Like Issa, her tone is playfully self-ironic; instead of shaking a fist at the universe—instead of complaining about the loss of youth that can never return—Hall opts for the comic gesture of letting go and laughter.

In this next example, Tim Gardiner finds humor at the bottom of a glass.

> pub philosophy . . .
> by the fifth pint
> world peace
> —Tim Gardiner

Issa wrote many haiku about sake drinking, most of which manifest the same joking tone as Gardiner's poem.

>   drunk on sake
>   he yanks
>   the radish[45]

Sakenomi-dono ("Mr. Drunkard") pulls up a radish, but—we can easily imagine—he does so quite awkwardly. The alcohol in his bloodstream has changed his consciousness and dexterity in a funny way, especially when observed by a sober person. Adopting the same tactic, Gardiner alludes to a spirited conversation at a pub on the serious topic of war and how to end it. The reader realizes that the "peace plan" cooked up over pints of beer or ale is most likely no steadier than the legs of an inebriated radish-pulling farmer. Just as Hall joins Issa in laughing at her own aging process, Gardiner joins Issa in laughing at his own drunken incompetence. Gardiner's haiku, however, goes farther to touch upon a troubling human reality. The reader may smile at the certitude arrived at by the fifth pint, but the poem has deep implications. The human inhabitants of our beautiful planet seem always so much readier to choose mutual destruction than peaceful coexistence. Sadly, the haiku hints that world peace may *only* exist inside the dreams of drunkards.

Robert B. McNeill discovers a surprising and amusing connection between a lawn mower and cicadas.

> starting the mower
> a thousand cicadas
> fall in love
> —Robert B. McNeill

My maternal grandmother played piano and swore that when she played with her window open, birds would gather in a nearby tree to sing along. McNeill notices a similar connection between human and animal when the firing up of his mower seems to instigate an excited crescendo in the chorus of chirring cicadas. Since the cicadas are males calling for mates, McNeill proposes the absurdity that the sound of the machine, too, has become a love call—and that a thousand cicadas are singing out their shrill, amorous response. The conceit is silly, but on a deeper level this comic haiku whispers a cosmic secret: ours is a shared planet on which humans and animals equally belong, respond to one another, and perhaps, even, can be (or must be?) lovingly connected.

Greg Longenecker's haiku about an abandoned farm is also silly on the surface while, deeper, disclosing a truth—in this case, a somber one.

> abandoned farm
> the dandelions make
> their own wishes
> —Greg Longenecker

With no people around, especially no children, there is no one to blow the dandelion seeds and make wishes. Instead, Longenecker claims, "the dandelions make/ their own wishes." This notion raises a smile, but the scene of abandoned property with dandelion puff-seeds scattering without human help—presumably blown by a wind—has profound emotional and intellectual connotations. I'm reminded of Bashō's penchant for writing haiku with *sabi*, a sense of the loneliness that permeates human existence. The family is absent, hinting that perhaps they lost their farm; they couldn't make it work; their wishes went unanswered. As with all fine haiku, the most important part of the poem isn't stated outright but gently implied.

In a verse by David Oates the humor is darker.

> womb gone
> she does art on the theme
> "scrambled eggs"
> —David Oates

Oates's poem isn't a cheap joke told at the expense of the woman in question. Because she chooses to make the most of her condition, mining it for ironic, artistic inspiration, his haiku celebrates the resiliency of her spirit—of the human spirit. This is spot-on Issa-like humor: not only accepting a tragic reality but rising above it to reach a higher plane of consciousness: of surrendering acceptance and laughter.

Poets who write like Issa learn to discover humor in ordinary, work-a-day life, as Perry L. Powell does in these next two examples.

> the bug man
> talking of his royal
> ancestry
> —Perry L. Powell

> missed deadline
> another programmer
> in the loop
> —Perry L. Powell

Powell comically exploits the proletarian bug exterminator's absurd claim to noble lineage. His pretentiousness is hilarious, since noblemen by definition needn't work with their hands, needn't handle dangerous chemicals, and certainly needn't make their living by destroying the lives of tiny fellow creatures. Or might they? Might the humor in this poem also be operating on a deeply satirical level? Powell might be implying that men of royal blood historically have achieved this status by treating generations of fellow human beings like cockroaches, crushing them underfoot. The arrogant bug man's remark is silly but, upon deeper reflection, possibly disturbing.

In his second haiku Powell offers insight into the life of a computer programmer. The two meanings of "in the loop" overlap nicely in the poem: because of a missed deadline, another programmer has been assigned to the project: "in the loop" both in the sense of having access to the information and physically, perhaps intrusively, adding his or her own lines of code to its loops of logic. Powell says nothing about how he feels about this assigned helper, but the reader can guess at his irritation and injured pride. Like all successful comedy, the situation is utterly relatable. One needn't be a computer programmer to understand how it feels to be chided for one's performance on the job and—adding insult to injury—having the boss assign a coworker to "help" complete one's project. In both of these examples, Powell reveals an Issa-like talent for finding humor in moments of everyday life: humor that beckons readers toward deeper reflection.

I'll close this lesson with just a few more examples of comic haiku to consider and to meditate on. Note how each of these poets discovers ironies and absurdities in ordinary life: in human psychology, in animal behavior, in the doings of adults, and in the play of children. Each of these poets is choosing a path of laughter and acceptance; each of them is writing like Issa.

> her sashay
> effective
> they follow
> —Patricia Wakimoto

hummingbird
trying to drink
from my red earrings
 —Dyana Basist

the old priest dines
his wine
just wine
 —David G. Lanoue

silver fish
despite your lovely name
squashed
 —Marietta Jane McGregor

gardening . . .
the cat too
sprays the flowers
 —Robert B. McNeill

lemonade stand—
a pair of 6-year olds
discuss the downturn
 —Robert B. McNeill

moving house
the old dog pisses
in new places
 —Gregory Piko

Lesson 4. BOLD SUBJECTIVITY: THE "I" HAS IT

THOUGH SOME GUIDES TO HAIKU advise poets to erase their personal lives as much as possible from their poems, striving for clean objectivity, Issa instructs us, by his example, to boldly expose the most intimate details and emotions of our lives. Many hundreds of his haiku include the words "I," "me," or "my," and many thousands more strongly suggest Issa's presence and active, personal involvement in scenes without explicitly saying so, as in the following examples.

> siesta work
> for the stepchild . . .
> picking brother's fleas[46]
>
> made with sooty paper
> the stepchild's kite
> easy to spot[47]

Readers familiar with Issa's biography will quickly conclude that the stepchild in these verses must be the poet; that they are memory pieces based on his troubled childhood. Even if, by chance, the sight of some other stepchild and not a memory of his own life happened to inspire one or both of these haiku, the fact that Issa continually describes himself as a stepchild throughout his work suggests that, on a deep level of interpretation, they are also self-portraits. When his father remarried, young Issa (then named Yatarō) was only eight years old. At age ten his stepmother Satsu gave birth to his half-brother, Senroku. According to Issa's later account in one of his journals, Satsu treated him horribly and forced him to take care of his little brother, the apple of her eyes. It's possible that Issa may have exaggerated Satsu's cruelty because when he wrote about it he was a middle-aged adult battling her for his share of his inheritance left by his father. However, we have no reason to doubt that losing his mother at age three and his life as a "stepchild" from the impressionable ages eight to fifteen emotionally scarred Issa, so that whenever he includes a stepchild in his poetry, even images of stepchild sparrows, he is reflecting on his own troubled childhood.

Ironically, Issa's most personal haiku convey his most universal messages. He certainly wasn't the world's only emotionally abandoned child. His self-portraits as such serve as portraits of millions of human beings who, as children, have been starved for parental kindness and love. In a similar way, when he writes about the deaths of his own loved ones—his mother, his father, his first wife, and their four children—Issa transforms this most personal grief into most universal artistic statements.

> splashing me
> the survivor . . .
> grassy dew[48]

> this world
> is a dewdrop world
> yes . . . but . . .[49]

He wrote the first poem on the day that he

gathered up the ashes of his father, who had just been cremated. The second one, perhaps his most famous haiku, reflects on the death of his toddler daughter Sato, by smallpox. In both poems (and many others about the deaths of family members and friends), dew serves as a metaphor for a fleeting, temporary life. Issa universalizes his private losses by making use of this conventional Buddhist symbol for transience: life is like a dewdrop that lasts only for a brief time until the morning sun burns it away. The poet's sorrow and heartbreak at lost "dewdrops" in this dewdrop world stand for everyone's sorrow and everyone's heartbreak, because everyone, sooner or later, loses people they love.

The second poem ends with the phrase, *nagara sari nagara*, which is often translated as "yet, and yet" (I have rendered it, "yes . . . but . . ."). Issa the Buddhist may understand that all things pass away in this temporary dewdrop world; that an enlightened person should not attempt to grasp at what cannot be kept (the "tragic gesture" discussed in the previous lesson). Even so, Issa the grieving father can't let go. Yes, this world may be evanescent with every thing and creature in it destined to fade to oblivion . . . *and yet!* This haunting "and yet . . ." speaks volumes not only about Issa's personal grief but also about a universal grief of all the inhabitants of a planet on which every living thing must die. Religion may attempt to provide solace—Buddhists advising nonattachment to the dewdrop world; Christians assuring that one's loved ones are "in a better place"—but the broken human heart that is both Issa's heart and everyone's heart cries out, inconsolably, "*AND YET!*"

In the previous lesson we saw how Issa lampoons his own aging process in haiku (recall the cat with good teeth "laughing" at the toothless poet). In other verses, such as the following, he contemplates his own death.

> when will it become
> a cricket's nest?
> my white hair[50]

> when I die
> guard my grave
> katydid![51]

Issa, being Issa, can't seem to write about his mortality without envisioning it as a cosmic joke: that his white hair will one day serve as a cozy nest for a cricket, or that a katydid will eventually sing over and "protect" his grave. Unlike his haiku about deceased loved ones featuring images of evaporating dewdrops and a feeling of emptiness and loss, Issa imagines his own demise with a tone of cheerful acceptance. He is alive on this earth for a short time, singing as best he can in the form of *haikai* poetry, and after his time is through, his song ends . . . but not the singing. Poet insects—crickets and katydids—will continue chirping and chirring. Life will abide.

Issa doesn't hesitate to personalize death, imagining *his* white hair as a cricket's nest and *his* grave as one being watched over by a katydid. Yet, we see again, his most personal poetic statements become his most universal. After all, every reader, too, will die someday, and if a reader is fortunate enough to do this after arriving at a ripe old age, he or she, too, will almost certainly experience physical changes such as the whitening (and loss) of hair. Issa thus speaks not only about himself in these poems but about all readers, all people. Each of us will die; our song will end . . . but the music, to repeat, will not.

James Dwyer anticipates his own death in a haiku in which he, like Issa, chooses humor and acceptance.

> after this birthday
> even gray skies
> are a gift
> —James Dwyer

Dwyer notes playfully that after *this* birthday (presumably not a small number), he looks forward to "gifts" quite different from those that he may have collected from family or friends on that day. Even gray skies will be among these future presents from the universe, he declares, expressing a feeling of gratitude for each new day, each new sky . . . even gloomy and overcast ones. The sky may be dark and cloudy, but the poet's heart will fill with joy, for it is the heart of an old man who knows that he is old and who realizes, profoundly, that every day left of life is a treasure. He is ready to unwrap those days, those gifts, one by one—savoring each until the last gift arrives.

Dwyer and Issa are certainly on the same page here both in their haiku style and in their deeper implications. Issa, too, proclaims in the following two haiku his joyful intention to capitalize on whatever precious time he has left on earth.

> once again
> I've managed not to die . . .
> blossoming spring[52]

> from this year on
> just carousing . . .
> this world's blossoms[53]

These poems were written seventeen years apart (in 1804 and 1821), but they express the same thought. The poet who knows that death will eventually come is determined to revel in the beauty of another new year, another blossoming spring. His joy and resolution to enjoy life in the second haiku are especially strong, since the previous winter he had suffered a stroke and a bout of partial paralysis. He uses the Japanese word *mōke*, "profit," to describe how he plans to make the most of his remaining days—a word choice that recalls the English idiom, "The rest is gravy." Like Dwyer, who looks forward even to gray skies, Issa vows to devote the remainder of his life, "from this year on," to reveling in the fragile beauty of this world—good advice for a haiku poet but also for his readers, whether or not they are poets themselves.

In some cases Issa writes himself into his verses in such a way that it would seem that he is making light of his poverty.

> hole in the wall
> pretty
> my year's first sky[54]

> hole in the wall—
> my harvest moon
> comes in[55]

> looking pretty
> in a hole in the paper door . . .
> Milky Way[56]

Issa filled his journals with scores of haiku alluding to his status as "Shinano Province's Chief Beggar," living in a rundown "Trash Hut." In many of those poems, as in the above examples, he ironically finds that being poor can prove to be a lucky thing: the hole a wall or door allows one to view the sky on New Year's morning, the glorious moon, and Heaven's dazzling "river" of stars (the Milky Way). Issa truthfully was not rich, especially before age fifty when he finally settled back in the family home in Kashiwabara for a more stable, middle class existence. On one level, then, his references to his poverty are simply a reporting of the truth—actual or remembered. However, his message goes deeper than that. He uses the literary persona, Issa the Beggar, to convey universal lessons to his readers, including this plea: "Open yourself to this world's *true* treasures!"

In the twenty-first century, Stanford M. Forrester follows a similar path.

> autumn colors—
> the scarecrow's shirt
> nicer than mine
>   —Stanford M. Forrester

Forrester makes wry fun of his own relatively

shabby appearance, at least in this moment in which a scarecrow sports a nicer shirt than he does. Like Issa, Forrester hints of a thing more valuable than wealth or the fashionable clothing that signals wealth: the autumn colors. The bright colors of the changing leaves, perhaps complemented by or repeated in the color(s) of the scarecrow's shirt, are what *really* matter, not the amount of money in one's bank account or the niceness of one's shirt. Issa and Forrester dare to embrace the subjective in these poems while, in so doing, discovering universal truths embedded in their own lives.

Sometimes Issa sketches poetic self-portraits that are actually, in essence, explorations of Buddhism. His countless haiku about compassionate encounters with animals, some of which we looked at in Lesson 1, fall into this category. From time to time, however, he confesses that he has failed religiously, such as in the following poem.

> pesky flea
> caught in my hand
> become a Buddha![57]

Since becoming a Buddha is a euphemism for dying, Issa is confessing that he is violating the Buddha's injunction against taking life. He pinches and crushes the "pesky" insect, and then lamely attempts to justify his crime by claiming that he has mercifully hastened the flea toward a better incarnation and eventual Buddhahood. On one level, he humorously presents himself as a spiritual hypocrite, failing to manifest, in a moment of irritation, his customary tenderness for fellow creatures, even fleas. On a level of deeper signification, however, this admission of personal religious failure can be read as a general statement about the human condition and human imperfection—one of the main themes of the founder of Issa's particular sect of Pure Land Buddhism, Shinran.

Meik Blöttenberger, Issa-like, writes himself into his own haiku in which the personal also has broader meaning.

> saving a wasp
> in the birdbath
> this man I've become
> —Meik Blöttenberger

Issa admits to a lapse in compassion, killing a flea; Blöttenberger portrays the opposite: a moment of successfully respecting life. Both haiku evoke deeper lessons. Blöttenberger notices and acknowledges, as if surprised by the revelation, "this man I've become." The man he was before would have probably let the wasp drown, but not today. Private gestures are loaded with public significance; readers reflecting on these haiku about killing and not killing might be led to contemplate and examine their own treatment of other living things on the planet.

Gregory Piko also doesn't shy away from self-scrutiny in haiku.

> a finch in the sun
> I am well
> after all
> —Gregory Piko

Nor does Charlotte Digregorio.

> pruning
> the bonsai . . .
> my knotty life
> —Charlotte Digregorio

In the act of creating these haiku both poets learn something about themselves in relation to nature, and both boldly allow these deeply felt discoveries to become the focus of attention. For Piko the sunlit vision of a finch somehow triggers the realization that, "I am well/ after all," while Digregorio's intent pruning of a presumably knotty bonsai unlocks a sudden insight into her own life. It, too, is knotty: difficult to trim, impossible to reduce to simple, straight lines.

These profoundly introspective poems are quite reminiscent of those of Issa, for whom the experience of nature often triggered revelations of his own life and how it felt to be living it.

> autumn wind—
> Issa's heart and mind
> stirring[58]

Since *kokoro* can mean "heart" or "mind" in Japanese, this haiku might be translated, "autumn wind—/ the mind of Issa is thinking," or "autumn wind—/ the heart of Issa is feeling." Both would be correct yet incomplete, hence my translation. For a poet who habitually makes his personal life the stuff of poetry, this enigmatic haiku is perhaps his most inward-gazing self-portrait. What thoughts and feelings might be stirring inside Issa as the chilly autumn wind wafts over him? Are they thoughts and feelings about human mortality, perhaps, given his customary linkage of autumn to the idea of time ticking away toward death? Issa leaves this mystery for individual readers to ponder and solve for themselves, just as Piko allows *his* readers to wonder about and speculate on why he suddenly feels that he is "well" upon spotting the finch; and just as Digregorio lets *her* readers employ the exquisite image of life as a difficult-to-trim bonsai tree as a sort of meditative mandala to inspire contemplation of their own "knotty" (or "naughty"?) existences.

Sometimes Issa's subjective poetry expresses regret for how his life has turned out.

> if only for a day
> to have my own house!
> plum blossoms[59]

Written at a time when he was poor and still living in exile from the family home in Shinano, his return still being blocked by his stepmother Satsu, Issa felt great disappointment at age forty-two for not having his own home in the world with a pretty plum tree blooming in its little, trimmed garden. While deeply personal and autobiographical, the poem (again) can be read as an expression of a common human experience. All readers may not have been literally homeless in their lives, but most *have* probably yearned for something better at some point and have harbored deep regrets.

> red maple buds—
> how long since
> we've last made love?
> —Elliott Nicely

> quiet evening
> the scars we carry
> begin to itch
> —Jill Lange

> another place
> I've sinned
> boarded-up hotel
> —David G. Lanoue

These twenty-first century poets (I included) follow in Issa's footsteps, making our personal disappointments and failings the focus of haiku. Petar Tchouhov reflects on a disappointment in his life in quite extreme terms that bring to mind not only fairy tales but Issa's biography.

> wind and rain
> I would accept even
> an evil stepmother
> —Petar Tchouhov

Cinderella and Issa at least had *someone*, though evil. Tchouhov, by implication, has no mother at all in the world. He appears in the moment emotionally naked: vulnerable to the pitiless elements of wind and rain that psychologically can stand for so much more.

All of the poets in the above examples write the kind of highly personal haiku that many self-proclaimed "experts" would summarily reject.

Master Issa, however, gives us license to go beyond safe, sanitary objectivity: to courageously expose the inner worlds of our hearts and minds.

> first blossoms—
> he identifies
> as bisexual
> —Nicholas M. Sola

> dandelion fluff . . .
> I have told you
> a hundred times
> —Diane Allen Hemingway

> dreams of Fuji . . .
> I awake to a heap
> of dirty clothes
> —Tim Gardiner

> another winter
> my lap empty
> of cat
> —Terri L. French

> robin's egg blue
> how my father would have loved
> my son
> —Robyn Hood Black

In Lesson 2 we found that it is a brave thing to set aside our grownup desire to sound educated and smart, daring instead to perceive and write with the child's mind that still abides inside each of us, usually kept locked away. Similarly, in this lesson Issa calls us to do a risky thing: to reveal the deepest reality of who we are. Art can indeed be risky, and haiku, of course, is art. As you prepare to write your own verses of subjectivity, just remember that any experience that you have had and will write about might possibly touch readers who have gone through something similar. The private, in art, becomes public. Dare to write highly personal poetry of which some readers will say, with gratitude in their hearts for seeing it on the page with stark clarity, "Hey, that's *my* story!"

If you can manage this, you will be writing like Issa.

Lesson 5. IMAGINE GOING DEEPER

MANY POETS AND SOME EDITORS of journals dislike so-called "desk-ku": haiku dreamed up as works of pure imagination. Such writers and readers much prefer haiku to erupt from raw, genuine sensations and feelings—and I count myself as one of those writers and readers. However, this is not to say that I consider haiku to be *merely* versified field notes on life, unaltered by a poet's imagination. Many years of translating and pondering Issa have led me to a more nuanced understanding.

Issa had no qualms about revising and radically re-imagining his haiku, but he didn't pull his revisions out of thin air—that is, without consideration of, or relation to, real experiences from real life. A series of poems about a Great Buddha illustrates how he worked.

> 1813:
> in the great bronze
> Buddha's nose chirping . . .
> sparrow babies[60]

> 1814:
> from the great bronze
> Buddha's nostrils . . .
> morning fog[61]

1818:
from the great bronze
Buddha's nose . . .
soot-sweeping[62]

1822:
from the great bronze
Buddha's nose . . .
a swallow![63]

When he recorded these verses in his journal, Issa was staying in his home province of Shinano, hundreds of kilometers away from Japan's two most enormous bronze Buddhas at Kamakura and Nara. Since his reference to a Great Buddha would naturally lead his original readers to picture one of these two famous statues, the moments depicted in these four haiku, if they actually occurred, probably occurred in the past, given Issa's geographic location at the time of composition. However, one wonders: Is it likely that Issa *actually* experienced so many different things emerging from a Great Buddha's nose: the sound of chirping sparrow babies, an exhalation of fog, black clouds of soot, and that sudden swallow? While it is quite possible that the first image was based on direct experience, "recollected in tranquility" (to borrow William Wordsworth's phrase), it seems more than likely that the later emanations from the great nose were pure inventions, imagined at a desk.

By incessantly revising—trying out new combinations of remembered experiences—Issa ultimately arrived at his masterpiece poem of 1822 in which the Great Buddha sneezes forth . . . a swallow!

This series of haiku affords us a peek inside Cup-of-Tea's creative process. We can safely assume that all of the images in them are grounded in authentic, deeply perceived and deeply felt experiences; Issa's memories without doubt included indelible images of encounters with baby sparrows, morning fog, soot-sweepers, and swallows. His creative process involved coupling these images with that of the Great Buddha's great nose, as if restlessly trying to reach a deeper truth. In the first version, he juxtaposed the vast, ponderous statue with chirping baby sparrows. Other experiments followed, in which he substituted clouds of fog, then clouds of soot, as if striving for a more ethereal, then comical, feeling. Still, he wasn't satisfied. In the end, digging deep, he finally hit upon the image of a quick, fleeting bird bursting from Buddha's nostril, thereby creating one of the best haiku of his life: one that (in my reading of it) encapsulates in a single breath what it means to be alive on this planet: amazement, exuberance, and a precious beauty born of transience.

Since we don't have four versions for every poem in Issa's vast canon, we have no way of telling which images in them may have flowed from unique experiences and which ones involved the imaginative reshuffling of experiences. As noted in Lesson 3, many of Issa's most striking comic haiku appear to be examples of "found" humor: the kind of cosmic jokes that are just too good to be made up. Nevertheless, these Great Buddha verses indicate that he also grants his followers (that would be us) permission to recombine our past experiences in the service of reaching deeper and deeper for meaning.

Consider the following two haiku by Issa and reflect on the kind of perceptual imagination that made them possible.

> on the morning frost
> the blacksmith's sparks
> spurting[64]
>
> dangling
> in the yellow roses
> the bull's balls[65]

American poet Robert Bly speaks of the surprising "leaps" from image to image that, he believes, is a core quality of powerful poetry.[66] These two haiku indeed leap in Bly's sense of the term: from frost to spurting sparks, from yellow roses to a bull's testicles. Issa's imagination is fluid and nimble, but always grounded in real experiences of a real universe. In the first poem, he invites us to contemplate the relationship of frost and fire, cold and hot, death and life, inertia and the vigorous energy of a blacksmith's hammer-wielding arm. In the second poem, he presents us with startling, side-by-side images of flowers and balls, thus coaxing us to reflect on and wonder about the occult connections between female and male, yin and yang, and about the sacred mystery of fertility.

Petar Tchouhov, Nicholas M. Sola, and Marilyn Fleming all dare to leap—and leap far—within the confines of one-breath poetry.

> All Souls' Day
> I open my father's
> black umbrella
> —Petar Tchouhov

> autumn night—
> goose bumps
> above the bra clasp
> —Nicholas M. Sola

> I have been
> a dead thing—
> darkling winter
> —Marilyn Fleming

These poets soar from image to image, idea to idea, feeling to feeling—making the experience of reading their haiku true adventures of the heart and mind. Equally adventurous are Ludmila Balabanova and Michael Dylan Welch.

> poppies
> the earth remembers
> its heart of fire
> —Ludmila Balabanova

> sun through the rain . . .
> a fox is getting married
> in my dream
> —Michael Dylan Welch

The above five haiku are exceedingly powerful; each one leaps, and each one unfolds a bit more with each re-reading, each re-experiencing of their visual and emotional shifts. As you read and contemplate them, notice what the poets have accomplished through their bold, experience-grounded imaginations. I could write many pages about what each of these haiku are inducing *me* to see, feel, and wonder about—but this time, I won't.

This time, I'll leave the analysis to you.

***

Bly's concept of leaping derives from the subjective experience of juxtaposition. Although Richard Gilbert explores several types of disjunctions within haiku, citing juxtaposition as merely one of an array of possible semantic moves, juxtaposition is without doubt a key tool in Issa's poetic toolbox.[67] His normal method of constructing a haiku involves the presentation of Image A followed immediately by Image B. Reading such a poem, one pictures the first image, then mentally "leaps" to picture the second. In the silence that follows this experience of imagining, a skillful reader will take a bit of time to contemplate A and B side by side, reflecting on what the move from the one to the other might signify, emotionally and intellectually.

This leap is actually a plunge, like Bashō's famous frog into the old pond: a dive into the deeper implications of a moment.

> in this world
> over hell . . .
> viewing spring blossoms[68]

In this haiku Issa presents the image of hell (that is, the Buddhist hell, mercifully not eternal) alongside an image of spring blossoms, most likely cherry blossoms, since *hana* can mean cherry blossoms in the shorthand of haiku. The resulting juxtaposition is quite dramatic: darkness and suffering below, brilliance and revelry above. The image of afterlife misery intensifies the preciousness of the present moment of life, beauty, and enjoyment. If only for a short time, Issa suggests, this world has become hell's exact opposite; this world has become a paradise.

In other haiku Issa's strategy of juxtaposition and leaping is more complex.

> spring peace—
> a mouse licking up
> Sumida River[69]

Here, he sets up two juxtapositions: first, the image of a peaceful spring day alongside that of a drinking mouse. Then, he nests a second juxtaposition inside the haiku's second part: a great river to contrast with the tiny mouse. One might choose to find delight in the absurdity of a mouse aspiring to drink a river. Or, one might instead choose to find in the poem a reflection of one's own existence: how each of us is so miniscule, so fleeting, in a universe so amazingly vaster than us, flowing on and on.

Consider the following twenty-first century haiku and the inner journeys that their juxtaposed images make possible for readers.

only peanuts
in the mixed nuts can—
cold spring
    —Anna Cates

ants
making mountains
out of mountains
    —Autumn Noelle Hall

summer's bees
frozen
into winter stars
    —Stuart Bartow

Anna Cates presents an image of a mixed nuts can that has been picked clean of its special or exotic contents, leaving behind only the ordinary peanuts. From this disappointing image she leaps (in Bly's sense) to the seasonal reality of "cold spring"—another implied disappointment, for winter's cold is lingering when it has no right to, calendar-wise. Her images alone express, by their juxtaposition, the monotony of a winter that is refusing to release its icy grip. Following Issa, Cates's darkly humorous poem leaves much to the reader's imagination. If we decide to picture only one nut eater, the present disappointment has been self-inflicted. However, if we choose to imagine another person who has had access to the mixed nuts and who has devoured the "good ones," the coldness of the spring perhaps reflects the insensitivity of that other resident of the house . . . maybe a spouse?

    Autumn Noelle Hall juxtaposes "mountains" of anthills with real mountains, noting that the smaller mountains are being built, grain by grain, from the substance of the bigger ones. Perhaps lurking behind her playful leap from microcosm to macrocosm is a reversal of the English expression, "Making a mountain out of a molehill"? Either way, the shift in perspective is delightful and leads to deeper reflection on the importance of small, almost invisible creatures and processes. The great mountain and the tiny one are seamlessly, organically connected.

Stuart Bartow also leaps dramatically in his haiku: from a "before" image of summer bees to an "after" one of those same bees "frozen/ into winter stars." The cycle of the year and the cycle of life are compressed provocatively into six words. The imagination leaps from summer to winter, from birth to death, from bees to stars. As in Hall's haiku, another shift is one of smallness to vastness, from tiny bundles of life on planet Earth to the awesome expanse of the cosmos. From bee to star is a long leap, indeed. Bartow invites us to take that leap with him, in our minds, and to contemplate for ourselves what the journey means.[70]

To write like Issa one needs to rely not only on one's intimate sensory encounters with the universe, but also, sometimes, to combine those experiences to create powerful and evocative juxtapositions that lead to deeper insights. Barbara Snow and Ludmila Balabanova certainly have absorbed this lesson from Issa and have incorporated it into their haiku art. First, consider this example from Snow.

> a glint of tinsel
> in a high corner web
> epiphany
> —Barbara Snow

Snow's haiku begins with an interesting first juxtaposition: the human reality of the Christmas holidays alongside a spider's reality of web-weaving and stalking. From these two images she jump-cuts to a third: the semantically loaded word, "epiphany." On one level, she might be referring to the Christian Feast of the Epiphany, celebrated in early January. On this day she has noticed that a silver strand of tinsel from the Christmas tree has somehow migrated up into a high corner of the room, where now it dangles, caught in the web. The image directly recalls a haiku by Issa, also written in winter, in which the poet offers words of friendly assurance to his own "corner spider" (cited earlier; see Note 12).

> corner spider
> rest easy, my soot-broom
> is idle

Snow's haiku implies that the Christmas spirit of peace and love extends, in the home, even to a spider. The fact that its web, too, sports a glittering holiday decoration reinforces the notion that the arachnid is part of the family, participating, even if unconsciously, in family life. So far, the poem would be an excellent example for our Lesson 1, given its implied compassion for, and feeling of connection to, a fellow creature. Other meanings of epiphany, however, inspire the kind of imaginative leap that makes Snow's haiku also ideal for the present lesson. "Epiphany" can signify both a manifestation of divinity and a sudden revelation. The haiku thus could hint that the spider, too, contains a spark of the divine within it—and, if this is so, the haiku might affirm a belief that all creatures carry such a spark inside. God incarnates in the Christ Child; God incarnates in a spider. The haiku could further suggest that the glint of tinsel in the corner spider's web has triggered an "Aha!" moment for the poet: "epiphany" in the sense of discovery. The exact nature of her epiphany is left tactfully undefined. Snow, Issa-like, allows her readers to meditate for themselves on her intriguing juxtapositions, the leaps between, and the deeper truths that these leaps might reveal.

Like Snow's haiku, this next one by Ludmila Balabanova could also serve as an example of Lesson 1's compassionate vision. But also like Snow's, its imagery involves a powerful imaginative leap as well.

> blown dandelions . . .
> now a sparrow
> calls me "Mom"[71]
> —Ludmila Balabanova

Balabanova moves from "blown dandelions" to a sparrow chirping the surprise that the poet is "Mom," a revelation reminiscent of one of Issa's haiku, addressed to birds.

> wake up! wake up! my children—
> swallows, pigeons,
> sparrows[72]

Balabanova, like Snow, experiences an epiphany in the moment, and she invites her readers to experience one as well, if they are willing to soar along with her from the image of dandelion seeds scattering in air to a baby sparrow calling her "Mom." Each reader will need to find his or her own meanings in this journey of heart and mind. My own first feeling/thought is that the poem is a celebration of trust: seeds trust in the wind, and the baby sparrow—perhaps fallen out of its nest?—innocently and utterly trusts in its new mother. A possible discovery at journey's end (at least in my reading of the poem in *this* moment) is that the poet is *in essence* the sparrow's mother, and that the sparrow is *in fact* the poet's responsibility. Life on planet Earth is a family affair.

How can a poem so short say so much? Issa answers in this way: if you leave at least a crack between your images—or perhaps a canyon, or perhaps a vast, starry expanse—your readers will be invited to cross that gap, that canyon, that expanse with their imaginations, aided by personal memories, feelings, insights, associations, and dreams. Balabanova once proclaimed that a haiku is "an invitation to the reader to achieve his own enlightenment."[73] The gaps between images that beckon a reader to take imaginative leaps make this kind of individualized enlightenment possible.

Write like Issa. Let your imagination leap and soar, and invite your readers along for the ride.

Lesson 6. ANSWER ISSA IN KIND

BRITISH CLERIC AND WRITER Charles Caleb Colton, a younger contemporary of Issa, famously opined, "Imitation is the sincerest [form] of flattery."[74] The haiku poets of early modern Japan certainly agreed with Colton's sentiment. Bashō expressed his admiration for ancient Chinese poets by imitating their lines and images in his haiku, and later haiku poets showed their high esteem for Bashō by writing imitations of *his* verses. Issa was one of those poets. Bashō's most famous one-breath poem depicts an old pond with a frog jumping into it.

> old pond—
> a frog-jumping-into-water
> sound[75]
>   —Bashō

On the occasion of a visit to the ruins of Bashō's hut, Issa wrote:

> old pond—
> "let me go first!"
> jumping frog[76]

Issa not only expressed his respect for Bashō by imitating and poetically answering particular compositions of his, such as this one; he tacitly acknowledged, through the act of imitation, Bashō's authority and influence as a teacher of haiku.

When I invited poets to submit Issa-inspired haiku for inclusion in this book, I discovered that several of them are continuing the tradition of writing poems to answer particular, well-known haiku. Just as Issa learned from Bashō and put that learning to work in his sometimes playful, sometimes serious variations on the master's haiku, poets today are answering Issa in kind. For example, Issa wrote, quite famously:

> little snail
> inch by inch, climb . . .
> Mount Fuji[77]

Jessica Tremblay and Petar Tchouhov have answered him as follows.

> quickly, quickly,
> an ant climbs a postcard
> of Mount Fuji
> —Jessica Tremblay

> so far away
> from Mount Fuji—
> a dead snail
> —Petar Tchouhov

Tremblay's haiku, written in both French and English versions, is a funny parody that becomes even funnier when one takes into account the fact that Issa's expression, *soro-soro*, which I translate as "inch by inch," is normally rendered in English with the words, "slowly, slowly." Her contrarian ant "quickly, quickly" climbs the postcard image of the great mountain: a wonderful transformation of the original poem. I don't know if Tremblay was aware when she wrote this homage that Issa's snail actually ascended a small replica of Mount Fuji in a Buddhist temple's garden, not the real mountain. Whether she was or not, for readers who know this fact her answer verse becomes even more interesting: both Issa's snail and Tremblay's ant are physically distant from the real Fuji, climbing representations of Fuji, not Fuji itself. And our minds, as we imagine both poems, accompany the two pilgrims—slow snail, quick ant—climbing our own mental images of these images of Mount Fuji. Issa had fun encouraging the snail to patiently conquer a three-dimensional mock-up of Fuji; Tremblay has fun extolling her ant to conquer a two-dimensional duplicate. Tremblay's humorous imitation nevertheless reminds readers of the deeply spiritual implications of Issa's original poem: how it can inspire readers to reflect on what it means to be alive in this vast world, engaged in a long and seemingly endless quest for enlightenment. Some of us creep along; some of us run like hell.

Tchouhov's answer poem goes far beyond humorous parody. In it, he conjures a memory of Issa's original haiku, hence a memory of its original, spiritual message of slow, patient progress moving toward a lofty awakening—but he sets this memory against a shockingly different presentation of the snail and the mountain. One is dead; the other is "far away." There's no enlightenment here, no spiritual advancement. Dark in its implications, Tchouhov's poem is a masterful response to Issa's.

We could have included this next poem by Issa in Lesson 2 as an illustration of childlike vision.

> snow melting—
> the village brimming over . . .
> with children![78]

Robert Henry Poulin answers it with:

> deep snow
> and the village children
> all under roof
> —Robert Henry Poulin

Poulin's haiku can be viewed as a winter prequel for Issa's poem of arriving spring: a "before" image to precede Issa's "after." With the snow too deep to play outside, the children of the village find themselves cooped up miserably in their cramped, smoky homes. Instead of energy, excitement, and clamor, the village—from an outside perspective—remains cold, snowbound, motionless, and silent. The haiku is strong by itself, but when read with Issa's poem in mind, this array of contrasting seasons, images, and moods creates a wonderful effect. Poulin invites readers to visualize his poem and Issa's side-by-side: a portrait of deep winter stasis next to one that celebrates the explosive exuberance of spring.

Rick Tarquinio writes a haiku that in its surface details appears radically different from Issa's poem about children overrunning a village. However, if one pays close attention to Tarquinio's words and structure, some resemblances emerge.

> sudden rain
> flooding the marsh
> with frogsong
> —Rick Tarquinio

As in Issa's haiku, Tarquinio begins with a wet, natural event: "sudden rain" in place of "snow melting." This rain is evidently a spring rain, in light of the fact that the singing of frogs is a spring seasonal reference in Japanese haiku. In the middle phrases of both poems, places are being flooded: a village in Issa's case, and a marsh in Tarquinio's. Finally, each poet caps his work with a surprising revelation as to what exactly is flooding village and marsh: Issa's "children" and Tarquinio's "frogsong." Not only are the revelatory structures of the poems basically identical, the feelings that they evoke are almost the same as well. In both poetic scenes, spring's gushing water gives rise to gushing, springtime joy. Whether consciously or unconsciously, Tarquinio's haiku answers Issa's.

When Lynn Halley Allgood submitted the following haiku as an Issa-inspired example, I had to laugh. It's funny by itself, but when read in connection with a certain haiku by Issa, it becomes hilarious.

> from the giant
> donut comes
> a butterfly
> —Lynn Halley Allgood

Huge, donut-shaped signs like the ones that advertise Randy's Donuts in Southern California remain impressive, bigger-than-life, roadside apparitions, kitschy remnants from the 1950s. Allgood's haiku has all the key elements of a comic verse, Issa-style, with its jarring juxtapositions of huge/small, human-made/natural, artifact/creature . . . and many more odd pairings could be listed. These incongruities raise a smile, but what makes Allgood's poem laugh-worthy is its sly echoing of a haiku by Issa that we examined earlier:

> from the great bronze
> Buddha's nose . . .
> a swallow!

Both poems overflow with comic juxtapositions, but when considered together even more juxtapositions delightfully arise, the Great Buddha versus Great Donut being the most prominent. The imaginative journey from Great Buddha to Great Donut is a journey from Japan to America, from past to present, from the sublimely spiritual to the crassly commercial. Emerging from these oversized artifacts of culture are, respectively, a swallow and a butterfly, reminding us that what *really* matters—emerging dramatically from a nostril or a donut hole—is precious life itself: tiny, vulnerable, yet breathlessly impressive. Like all great answer poems, Allgood's is most interesting when considered alongside the earlier poem that it answers. The two together create a synergistic effect wherein the whole equals more than the mere sum of parts. One plus one, in this situation, equals three.

After he lost his beloved first wife Kiku, Issa obviously, deeply missed her. He wrote several haiku on this subject, including the following.

> if only she were here
> for nagging . . .
> tonight's moon![79]

He prefaced this poem in his journal with the explanation: "My fault-finding old wife passed away this year." Two centuries later, Robert Henry Poulin writes a ghostly echo of Issa's words:

> the moon tonight
> has a new face
> with you gone
> —Robert Henry Poulin

Poulin pays homage to Issa through creative imitation, connecting the grief for an absent someone with the dazzle of "tonight's moon." The emotion in these haiku runs deep. Something about the cold, ethereal light in the night sky intensifies a sensation of emptiness left in a heart when a dear one has departed.

Gregory Piko also honors Issa by means of allusive imitation.

> golden buddha
> a woman sleeps
> knees spread wide
> —Gregory Piko

The poem recalls Issa's:

> harvest moon—
> sitting cross-legged
> like Buddha[80]

In Issa's poem a moon-gazer, perhaps the poet himself, sits in an appropriately meditative, Buddha-like posture, as he contemplates the splendor of the harvest moon. We can assume, given the cultural context of early modern Japan, that the person meditating in the moonlight is a man. Piko presents a woman instead, and instead of showing her on a path toward spiritual awakening, he shows her sleeping. Her "knees spread wide" is a direct echo of Sam Hamill's translation of this haiku in which he describes the poet's sitting position with exactly this phrase.[81] Perhaps the woman in question in Piko's answer poem has been sitting in a Zen pose inside a temple, meditating before a golden image of Buddha; however, like countless Zen practitioners have done over the centuries, she has dozed off. Asleep, her posture hints more of indecency than of a spiritual exercise. Or, perhaps Piko is implying that the golden Buddha watches over his follower like a loving and protective father, blessing his sleeping child, in which case her eventual enlightenment might be assured. The two contrasting poems—Issa's original and Piko's answer—raise this and many other interesting possibilities of interpretation for readers to consider. Once again, the two haiku, side by side, create a powerful synergy. One plus one, in this case, might add up to ten.

This next answer poem, written by "Write like Issa" workshop participant Michael Henry Lee, creates an almost dizzying Hall of Mirrors effect: reflecting a haiku by Issa that, in turn, reflects a haiku by Bashō that, in turn, reflects an ancient Chinese verse by Du Fu.

> Arlington
> the uniformity
> of shadows
> —Michael Henry Lee

> among the footsteps
> of warriors . . .
> poppies[82]

"Arlington . . ." is a strong poem in its own right, with its image of the shadows of gravestones lined up with military precision, their "uniformity" slyly calling to mind the uniforms that the occupants of the graves once wore. The white stone markers at Arlington National Cemetery stand at perfect attention, row after row, in a field of trimmed green grass shaded by occasional trees: a tranquil, natural, present-day setting that contrasts eerily with the remembered violence that has filled so many graves. The thunder of guns and the screams of the dying are silenced now; what remains, Lee notes, are just shadows stretching over grass with unbending, heartbreaking uniformity.

Read alongside the haiku by Issa that inspired it, this rich and troubling poem achieves an even deeper resonance. Issa is standing (or imagining himself standing) in a battlefield of an earlier time, where armies of samurai once clashed with swords, spears, and steel-tipped arrows. In this place where warriors fought and died, poppies now bloom, reminding me of John McCrae's 1915 poem about a World War I battlefield, that begins with the haunting lines, "In Flanders fields the poppies blow/ Between the crosses, row on row . . ." After the carnage of war, McCrae (who could not have known Issa's haiku), observes, as Issa did a century earlier, fragile symbols of hope and peace growing and unfurling: the poppies.

Issa's haiku, as I mentioned, is an answer to one of Bashō's, also written about an ancient battlefield.

> summer grasses . . .
> all that remains
> of warriors' dreams[83]

. . . and, as I describe in detail in *Issa and Being Human* (Chapter 4), Bashō's poem poignantly answers Du Fu's eighth-century Chinese verse about a conquered city returning to nature. Lee's terse, emotionally loaded haiku invites readers to imagine it alongside Issa's, alongside Bashō's, alongside Du Fu's . . . so many battles, so many war dead—but still the grass grows; still the poppies bloom. Is nature reassuring us that peace, in the end, will prevail? Or does nature mock the foolishness of a species that in every age, every place, finds the pretexts and means for our mutual slaughter? Lee's answer poem raises deep questions.

As a translator of Issa, many of my own attempts at haiku have been conscious or unconscious imitations of the great Cup-of-Tea. An example of a conscious answer to a particular poem by him is the following.

> after his lecture
> on Buddhism
> red-light Shinjuku

The bustling, neon-blazing neighborhood of Shinjuku in Tokyo is a center for nightlife, with erotic entertainment and plenty of "love hotels." In October of 2007, I had the honor of giving a talk on Issa and Pure Land Buddhism at the Higashi Honganji Temple in the Asakusa neighborhood of Tokyo. After that talk, not feeling at all sleepy, I caught a train to Shinjuku. My haiku humorously relates my experience of an abrupt transition from lofty intellectual heights to a more earthly realm. It directly answers this one by Issa:

> after winter prayers
> right away . . .
> a trip to Yoshiwara[84]

Someone in the scene (perhaps Issa) has been attending a prayer service at a Buddhist temple, chanting thanksgiving for Amida Buddha, who vowed to make rebirth in the Pure Land, hence enlightenment, possible even for the gravest of sinners. Immediately thereafter, this same person goes directly to old Edo's walled-in pleasure district, the Yoshiwara . . . presumably to sin! This jarring and humorous transition in Issa's haiku filled my mind as I wandered the neon-lit streets of Shinjuku that night, gawking—and provided the template for my own poem, written a few days later.

Answering Issa, I felt somehow close to him, as if I was momentarily seeing the world of my own experience through his eyes; as if I was creating the kind of haiku that, if he were me, he might have written. Maybe this is how Issa felt when he poetically answered Bashō . . .? When one writes an imitation poem, one joins a long literary tradition, absorbing what one's forbearers contributed to that tradition while adding new work that, if deemed usesful by future poets, might in turn be imitated and answered. We thus conclude our lessons with an exciting invitation.

Think like Issa; write like Issa; jump into the old pond of haiku tradition. Add your own ripples!

To make an answer poem, first you must select a haiku that, in your opinion, needs and deserves answering. You might thumb through the pages of this book or some other translation of Issa's haiku—in print or on the Web—until you find one that you feel inspired to imitate. Or, you might choose any one of the following verses, none of which, to my knowledge, has ever before spawned an answer poem. You could be the very first poet to do so.

***

evening gloom—
a fawn's spots
on the lily[85]

a katydid
in the scarecrow's gut
singing[86]

from the shade
of the poison plant . . .
pure water[87]

on flowering mustard
sitting so lightly . . .
a mouse[88]

letting clams
vomit mud . . .
a moonlit night[89]

tied to
the buck's antler . . .
a letter[90]

the stonecutter
chop-chops the mountain . . .
winter moon[91]

the child hugs
her cloth monkey . . .
hailstorm[92]

wind blows—
the wild boar's sleeping face
so innocent[93]

cats' love calls—
between them flows
Sumida River[94]

spring rain—
in my lover's sleeve
coins jingle[95]

without you—
this grove
is just a grove[96]

Conclusion: FOR THE SAKE OF HAIKU

> guard over haiku
> I beseech you!
> snow Buddha[97]

ISSA WROTE THE ABOVE VERSE in 1815, a little over two centuries ago. When I first read and translated it, I interpreted it to mean that he must have laid a haiku written on a slip of paper, or perhaps even his entire haiku journal, in the protective lap of a snow Buddha. Shokan Takashi Kondo, however, reads the poem differently. He believes that Issa is actually asking Buddha to guard over haiku poetry in general, more precisely, to guard over *haikai* in general: a term that refers both to what we today call haiku and to linked verse (*renku*), of which Kondo is a renowned master. This broader reading of the poem makes it far more interesting, far more important.

Who, today, will guard over the fragile blossom of haiku? Who will protect it against the threats of societal indifference to all forms of poetry, of selfish materialism, and of a widespread blindness to nature and to our absolute inclusion in it? Who will defend haiku against the heresy, rampant on the Worldwide Web, that this type of poetry consists of any random string of words tossed together in a 5-7-5 syllable pattern? And who will save it from perhaps well-meaning but sadly misguided editors who publish books of "haiku" filled with obtuse, abstract, and vapid language games? Instead of inviting readers into the intimacy of real experiences and the joy of real discoveries, such editors and the poets whom they champion threaten to rob haiku of its very essence.

Writing like Issa is not only fun or challenging or nourishing for the heart and mind; it's important.

Writing like Issa and sharing such poems with the world is a way (I believe, the *best* way) to protect haiku in difficult times.

I hope that this little book has inspired you to join with the snow Buddha, with Issa, with me, and with all the generous poets whose one-breath, Issa-like verses grace these pages. Together, we can—we will—guard over haiku.

We can—we will—answer Issa's call.

NOTES

1. 痩蛙まけるな一茶是に有り
   yasegaeru makeru na issa kore ni ari

   scrawny frog, hang tough!
   Issa
   is here

   蚤どもがさぞ夜永だろ淋しかろ
   nomi domo ga sazo yonaga daro sabishi karo

   for you fleas
   the night must be long . . .
   and lonely?

   These and all translations of Issa in this book are my own, based on original Japanese texts found in *Issa zenshū* (Nagano: Shinano Mainichi Shimbunsha, 1976-1979). All of my translations have been previously posted on my online archive, *The Haiku of Kobayashi Issa*.

2. 朝寒や蟾も眼を皿にして
   asa-zamu ya hiki mo manako wo sara ni shite

3. 鶏やちんば引々日の長き
   niwatori ya chinba hiki-hiki hi no nagaki

4. こほろぎの寒宿とする衾哉
   kōrogi no kanshuku to suru fusuma kana

5. やれ打な蝿が手をすり足をする
   yare utsuna hae ga te wo suri ashi wo suru

6. 鶏の小首を曲げる夜寒哉
   fuyugomori tori ryōri ni mo nembutsu kana

7. 夕月や鍋の中にて鳴田にし
   yūzuki ya nabe no naka nite naku tanishi

8. かたつぶり何をかせぐぞ秋の雨
   katatsuburi nani wo kasegu zo aki no ame

9. 夕雲雀どの松島が寝よいぞよ
   yū hibari dono matsushima ga ne yoi zo yo

10. 行々しどこが昔の難波なる
    gyōgyōshi doko ga mukashi no naniwa naru

11. 杭の鷺汝がとしはどう暮る
    kui no sagi nanji ga toshi wa dō kururu

12. Colpitt's haiku resembles one by Issa:

    隅の蜘案じな煤はとらぬぞよ
    sumi no kumo anjina susu wa toranu zo yo

    corner spider
    rest easy, my soot-broom
    is idle

    Issa reassures a spider; Colpitts reassures a fly. Note that Issa spells *kumo* with only one kanji.

13. かはほりに夜ほちもそろりそろり哉
    kawahori ni yahochi mo sorori-sorori kana

14. 乞食子がおろおろ拝む雛哉
    kojiki ko ga oro-oro ogamu hiina kana

15. "Ce n'est pas la pluie/ quelqu'un pleure cette nuit/ dans l'escalier." English translation by David G. Lanoue.

16. "Fête du quartier/ elle se maquille ce soir/ pour masquer les coups." English translation by David G. Lanoue.

17. "Нямах монети –/ пуснах в шапката на просяка/ въздишка." English translation by Ludmila Balabanova.

18. "Sin monedas la niña/ su mejor sonrisa/ para el mendigo." English translation by David G. Lanoue.

19. 重箱の銭四五文や夕時雨
    jūbako no zeni shi go mon ya yū shigure

20. 掛取が土足ふみ込むいろり哉
    kaketori ga dosoku fumi-komu irori kana

21. おのが里仕廻ふてどこへ田植笠
    ono ga sato shimaute doko e taue-gasa

22. 牢屋から出たり入つたり雀の子
    rōya kara detari ittari suzume no ko

23. 雀の子そこのけそこのけ御馬が通る
    suzume no ko soko noke soko noke o-uma ga tōru

24. See "Becoming a Child: Issa's Poetic Consciousness" in *Modern Haiku* 46.3 (Autumn 2015): 23-33; and Chapter 1, "Children," in *Issa and Being Human: Haiku Portraits of Early Modern Japan* (New Orleans: HaikuGuy.com, 2017) 12-30.

25. See Robin Carhart-Harris, "The Entropic Brain: A Theory of Conscious States Informed by Neuroimaging Research with Psychedelic Drugs," in *Frontiers in Human Neuroscience* (3 February 2014), Web.

26. "In gathering your vital energy to attain suppleness,/ Have you reached the state of a new-born babe?" (Chapter 10); "Learning consists in daily accumulating;/ The practice of Tao consists in daily diminishing . . ." (Chapter 48), from Lao Tzu, *Tao Teh Ching*, Tran. John C. H. Wu (Boston: Shambhala, 1990).

27. 牛もうもうもうと霧から出たりけり
    ushi mō mō mō to kiri kara detari keri

28. Greene's grammar, too, is childlike. Instead of "stars in the night sky/ appear to be . . ." he writes, "stars in the night sky/ appears to be . . ."

29. 犬の子の踏まへて眠る柳哉
    inu no ko no fumaete nemuru yanagi kana

30. 露の玉つまんで見たるわらべ哉
    tsuyu no tama tsumande mitaru warabe kana

31. 庭のてふ子が這へばとびはへばとぶ
    niwa no chō ko ga haeba tobi haeba tobu

32. 犬どもが蛍まぶれに寝たりけり
    inu domo ga hotaru mabure ni netari keri

33. 玉霰それそれ兄が耳房に
    tama arare sore sore ani ga mimi fusa ni

34. "Birke gefällt/ Holzstoß an der Wand/ Splitter im Daumen." English translation by Traude Veran.

35. 春風や大宮人の野雪隠
    haru kaze ya ōmiyabito no no setchin

36. 野はこせん見ることなかれみそさざい
    no hako sen miru koto nakare misosazai

37. 若草や今の小町が尻の跡
    wakakusa ya ima no komachi ga shiri no ato

38. 御仏の鼻の先にて屁ひり虫
    mi-hotoke no hana no saki nite hehirimushi

39. 屁くらべや芋名月の草の庵
    he kurabe ya imo meigetsu no kusa no io

40. Ōshiki Zuike, *Jinsei no hiai: Kobayashi Issa* (Tokyo: Shintensha, 1984).

41. 虫の屁を指して笑ひ仏哉
    mushi no he wo yubisashite warai-botoke kana

42. 留主にするぞ恋して遊べ庵の蝿
    rusu ni suru zo koi shite asobe io no hae

43. "любов/ върху тънката жица –/ два гълъба."
    English translation by Ludmila Balabanova.

44. 歯固は猫に勝れて笑ひけり
    hagatame wa neko ni katarete warai keri

45. 野大根酒呑どのに引れけり
    no daikon sake nomi dono ni hikare keri

46. 継つ子や昼寝仕事に蚤拾ふ
    mamakko ya hirune shigoto ni nomi hirou

    The word "brother" has been added to clarify the scene in light of Issa's biography.

47. すすけ紙まま子の凧としられけり
    susuke-gami mamako no tako to shirare keri

48. 生残る我にかかるや草の露
    ikinokoru ware ni kakaru ya kusa no tsuyu

49. 露の世は露の世ながらさりながら
    tsuyu no yo wa tsuyu no yo nagara sari nagara

    This haiku is a rewrite of one that Issa composed two years earlier, in 1817, to commemorate the one-year anniversary of the death of his firstborn child, the boy Sentarō. It has a one-word pre-script: "Grieving."

    露の世は得心ながらさりながら
    tsuyu no yo wa tokushin nagara sari nagara

    it's a dewdrop world
    surely it is . . .
    yes . . . but . . .

50. こほろぎの巣にはいつなる我白髪
    kōrogi no su ni wa itsu naru waga shiraga

51. 我死なば墓守となれきりぎりす
    ware shinaba haka mori to nare kirigirisu

52. 又土になりそこなうて花の春
    mata tsuchi ni narisokonaute hana no haru

53. ことしからまふけ遊びぞ花の娑婆
    kotoshi kara mōke asobi zo hana no shaba

54. 壁の穴や我初空もうつくしき
    kabe no ana ya waga hatsuzora mo utsukushiki

55. 壁穴に我名月の御出哉
    kabe ana ni waga meigetsu no oide kana

56. うつくしやしようじの穴の天の川
    utsukushi ya shōji no ana no ama no kawa

57. あばれ蚤我手にかかつて成仏せよ
    abare nomi waga te ni kakatte jōbutsu seyo

58. 秋の風一茶心に思ふやう
    aki no kaze issa kokoro ni omou yō

59. 一日も我家ほしさよ梅の花
    ichi-nichi mo waga ya hoshisa yo ume no hana

60. 大仏の鼻で鳴也雀の子
    daibutsu no hana de naku nari suzume no ko

61. 大仏の鼻から出たりけさの霧
    daibutsu no hana kara detari kesa no kiri

62. 大仏の鼻から出たり煤払
    daibutsu no hana kara detari susu harai

63. 大仏の鼻から出たる乙鳥哉
    daibutsu no hana kara detaru tsubame kana

64. 朝霜に野鍛冶が散火走る哉
    asa-jimo ni no kaji ga chiribi hashiru kana

65. 山吹にぶらりと牛のふぐり哉
    yamabuki ni burari to ushi no fuguri kana

66. Robert Bly, *Leaping Poetry: An Idea with Poems and Translations* (Pittsburgh: University of Pittsburgh Press, 1975; rpt. 2008).

67. Richard Gilbert, *The Disjunctive Dragonfly: A New Approach to English-Language Haiku* (Richard Gilbert, 2013).

68. 世の中は地獄の上の花見哉
    yo no naka wa jigoku no ue no hanami kana

69. 長閑や鼠のなめる角田川
    nodokasa ya nezumi no nameru sumida-gawa

    Issa wrote two other versions of this haiku, trying out different seasonal contexts. In addition to "spring peace," he used "spring breeze" and "spring rain." The "spring peace" version is his last.

70. Readers who quibble that Bartow has broken a rule of haiku by including two season words might be reminded that rules in art are meant to be broken—a truth that Issa embraced when he composed his own haiku that includes both blossoms (spring) and moon (autumn):

    月花や四十九年のむだ歩き
    tsuki hana ya shi jūku nen no muda aruki

    moon! blossoms!
    forty-nine years walking around
    a waste

71. "прецъфтели глухарчета . . ./ сега едно врабче/ ми казва 'мамо'." English translation by Ludmila Balabanova.

72. 起よ起よあこが乙鳥鳩すずめ
    oki yo oki yo ako ga tsubakura hato suzume

73. Quoted from "Between the West and the East," a presentation at the World Haiku Association Conference in Tenri, Japan, October 4, 2003. This talk was later published in *World Haiku 2005*, 95-104.

74. Aphorism #217 of *Lacon: Or, Many Things in Few Words: Addressed to Those Who Think* (1820-22). Later in the nineteenth century, Oscar Wilde added the rather snide qualification, "[. . .] that mediocrity can pay to greatness."

75. 古池や蛙飛び込む水の音
    furu ike ya kawazu tobikomu mizu no oto

    Quoted from *Matsuo Bashōshū* (Tokyo: Shogakukan, 1995) 1.146. English translation by David G. Lanoue.

76. 古池や先御先へととぶ蛙
    furu ike ya mazu o-saki e to tobu kawazu

77. かたつぶりそろそろ登れ富士の山
    katatsuburi soro-soro nobore fuji no yama

78. 雪とけて村一ぱいの子ども哉
    yuki tokete mura ippai no kodomo kana

79. 小言いふ相手もあらばけふの月
    kogoto yū aite mo araba kyō no tsuki

113

80. 名月や仏のやうに膝をくみ
    meigetsu ya hotoke no yō ni hiza wo kumi

81. *The Spring of My Life and Selected Haiku by Kobayashi Issa* (Boston & London: Shambhala, 1997) 145.

82. 兵が足の跡ありけしの花
    tsuwamono ga ashi no ato ari keshi no hana

83. 夏草や兵共が夢の跡
    natsukusa ya tsuwamono domo ga yume no ato

84. 十夜から直に吉原参り哉
    jūya kara sugu ni yoshiwara mairi kana

85. 夕闇やかのこ斑のゆりの花
    yū yami ya kanoko madara no yuri no hana

86. きりぎりすかがしの腹で鳴にけり
    kirigirisu kagashi no hara de naki ni keri

87. 毒草の花の陰より清水哉
    dokusō no hana no kage yori shimizu kana

88. 菜の花やふはと鼠のとまりけり
    na no hana ya fuwa to nezumi no tomari keri

89. 蛤の芥を吐する月夜かな
    hamaguri no gomi wo hakasuru tsuki yo kana

90. さをしかの角に結びし手紙哉
    saoshika no tsuno ni musubishi tegami kana

91. 石切のかちかち山や冬の月
    ishikiri no kachi-kachi yama ya fuyu no tsuki

92. ちりめんの猿を抱く子よ丸雪ちる
    chirimen no saru wo daku ko yo arare chiru

93. 風吹や猪の寝顔の欲げなき
    kaze fuku ya shishi no ne-gao no hoshige naki

94. 猫なくや中を流るる角田川
    neko naku ya naka wo nagaruru sumida-gawa

95. 春雨や妹が袂に銭の音
    harusame ya imo ga tamoto ni zeni no oto

96. 君なくて誠に多太の木立哉
    kimi nakute makoto ni tada no kodachi kana

97. はいかいを守らせ給へ雪仏
    haikai wo mamorase tamae yuki-botoke

PUBLICATION CREDITS

The following haiku first appeared elsewhere, as indicated.

"abandoned farm . . ." Greg Longenecker. *Cattails* 1 (2016).

"after the storm . . ." Rick Tarquinio. *Mostly Water* (Rick Tarquinio, 2015).

"after this birthday . . ." James Dwyer. *The Healing Muse* 16.1 (Fall 2016).

"all day I watch . . ." Dyana Basist. *Geppo* 41.3 (August 2016).

"All Souls' Day . . ." Petar Tchouhov. *Shiki Kukai* (December 2006). Web.

"another place . . ." David G. Lanoue. *Frogpond* 36.2 (2013).

"baby calf . . ." Robert Epstein. *Turkey Heaven: Animal Rights Haiku* (Robert Epstein, 2016).

"blown dandelions . . ." Ludmila Balabanova. *Motes in the Sunbeam* (Plovdiv: Jannet 45, 2007).

"Buddhist monk . . ." Nika. *Albatross* (1995).

"cold morning . . ." Petar Tchouhov. *Shiki Kukai* (March 2006).

"constipated . . ." Elliot Nicely. *Modern Haiku* 38.3 (2007)

"a finch in the sun . . ." Gregory Piko. *Frogpond* 34.3 (2011).

"gardening . . ." Robert B. McNeill. *Moonset* 5.1 (Spring/Summer 2009).

"a glint of tinsel . . ." Barbara Snow. *Shiki Kukai* (November 2009). Web.

"golden buddha . . ." Gregory Piko. *Blithe Spirit* 13.4 (2003).

"heat of the day . . ." Julie Warther. *Modern Haiku* 47.1 (Winter/Spring 2016).

"in the crook . . ." Elliiot Nicely. *White Lotus* 7 (2008).

"lemonade stand . . ." Robert B. McNeill. *Frogpond* 32.1 (2009).

"a 'Lost Dog' sign . . ." David G. Lanoue. *Frogpond* 27.2 (2004).

"love/ on a thin wire . . ." Ludmila Balabanova. *Dewdrops on the Weeds* (Sofia: Small Stations Press, 2016).

"night storm . . ." Petar Tchouhov. *Ginyu* 28 (October 2005).

"no coins . . ." Ludmila Balabanova. *Cricket Song* (Plovdiv: Jannett 45, 2002).

"not easily brushed off . . ." Julie Warther. Art of Haiku contest semifinalist, September 2016.

"the old black cat . . ." John Hawkhead. *Haiku Presence* 47 (December 2012).

"the old priest dines . . ." David G. Lanoue. *Modern Haiku* 30.1 (Winter/Spring 1999).

"open window . . ." Alan Summers. Runner-up, Snapshot Press's Haiku Calendar competetion (2001).

"poppies . . ." Ludmila Balabanova. *Motes in the Sunbeam* (Plovdiv: Jannet 45, 2007).

"plum blossom . . ." Deodhar, Angelee. *Haiku Canada Newsletter* 17.2 (June 2004).

"pruning/ the bonsai . . ." Charlotte Digregorio. *Frogpond* 34.1 (2011).

"quickly, quickly . . . " Jessica Tremblay. The French version won a prize in the Fujisan Haiku contest (2011).

"quiet evening . . ." Jill Lange. *Failed Haiku* (January 2016).

"red maple buds . . ." Elliott Nicely. *White Lotus* 9 (2009).

"relax, fly . . ." Sue Colpitts. Posted on *allpoetry.com* (2016).

"robin's egg blue . . ." Robyn Hood Black. *Acorn* 29 (Fall 2012).

"shooting gallery . . ." Petar Tchouhov. *Shamrock* 4 (2007).

"sky of stars . . ." J. Zimmerman. *Modern Haiku* (2014).

"so far away . . ." Petar Tchouhov. "Messages to Issa on the Tenth Anniversary of his Website" posted on *The Haiku of Kobayashi Issa* (May 2010).

"someone else . . ." David G. Lanoue. *Haiku: The Art of the Short Poem, A Film by Tazuo Yamaguchi* (2008).

"sudden rain . . ." Rick Tarquinio. *Mostly Water* (Rick Tarquinio, 2015).

"starting the mower . . ." Robert B. McNeill. *Modern Haiku* 45.1 (Winter/Spring 2014).

"summer rain . . ." Robert Witmer. *The Heron's Nest* 3 (September 2010). Wcb.

"where to house . . ." Robert Epstein. *Turkey Heaven: Animal Rights Haiku* (2016).

"wildflowers . . ." Julie Warther. *Tinywords* 16.1 (30 March 2016). Web.

"wind and rain . . ." Petar Tchouhov. *Public Republic* (2010).

"without coins the girl . . ." Gómez M., Victoria Eugenia. Original Spanish version in *Lunajera* (Cartago, Colombia: Rompesilencios Ediciones, 2012; rpt. 2015).

ABOUT THE AUTHOR

DAVID G. LANOUE is a professor of English at Xavier University of Louisiana. He is a cofounder of the New Orleans Haiku Society, an associate member of the Haiku Foundation, and former President of the Haiku Society of America. His books include translations (*Cup-of-Tea Poems; Selected Haiku of Kobayashi Issa, The Distant Mountain: The Life and Haiku of Kobayashi Issa,* and *Issa's Best: A Translator's Selection of Master Haiku*), criticism (*Pure Land Haiku: The Art of Priest Issa, Issa and the Meaning of Animals: A Buddhist Poet's Perspective,* and *Issa and Being Human: Haiku Portraits of Early Modern Japan*), and a series of "haiku novels," including *Haiku Guy, Laughing Buddha, Haiku Wars, Frog Poet,* and *Dewdrop World.* Some of his books have appeared in French, German, Spanish, Bulgarian, Serbian, and Japanese editions. He maintains *The Haiku of Kobayashi Issa* website, for which he translated 10,000 of Issa's haiku.

Made in the USA
Lexington, KY
18 September 2018